EXOTIC CARS

John Lamm

First published in 2008 by Motorbooks, an imprint of Quarto Publishing Group USA Inc., 400 First Avenue North, Suite 400, Minneapolis, MN 55401 USA

Motorbooks titles are also available at discounts in bulk quantity for industrial or sales-promotional use. For details write to Special Sales Manager at Quarto Publishing Group USA Inc., 400 First Avenue North, Suite 400, Minneapolis, MN 55401 USA.

To find out more about our books, join us online at www.motorbooks.com.

ISBN-13: 978-0-7603-3261-0

Editor: Peter Schletty
Designer: Laura Rade, LK Design Inc.

Printed in USA

On the cover: You won't hear many people call the Bugatti Veyron 16.4 beautiful, but no one denies that it has an exciting exterior shape. Up front is the traditional horseshoe-shaped grille that has been a part of every Bugatti. Out back is the tall spoiler needed to stabilize the car at speed.

On the frontispiece: Callaway has done Speedsters before, and they are a rare breed . . . and expensive, with a price tag just about $300,000. Pricey, but with a great bag of tricks, from the 616-horsepower supercharged V-8 to the lightweight carbon fiber road wheels.

On the title pages: It's all those vents that give the Porsche Turbo its serious, business look . . . and with good reason—actually the 480 reasons that represent the horsepower and the 457-to-502 that refer to the lb-ft of torque.

On the back cover, top: Ferrari's 50th anniversary gift to the automotive world was the F50. Built between 1995 and 1997, it was another example—like the F40 and Enzo—of Ferrari showing the best it could create. **Middle:** As in their race cars, McLaren's F1 LMs were built without the soundproofing used in the road machines. There is generous use of carbon-fiber for light weight. **Bottom:** The early Viper hits 60mph in less than 5 seconds. Vipers won their class in the 24 Hours of Le Mans from 1998 to 200, and an overall win the Rolex 24 at Daytona in 2000.

INTRODUCTION 4

CHAPTER 1 THE CLASSICS 6

CHAPTER 2 UP FRONT AUTOMOBILES 62

CHAPTER 3 MID-ENGINE ATTRACTION 170

INDEX 254

INTRODUCTION

You get in, sit down, buckle up, shut up, and start the engine. There's usually a healthy growl from the exhaust, so you know this isn't some wimp car. Snick the transmission into first gear via a classic shift lever or a paddle at the steering wheel. Onto the gas pedal, and off you go...quickly, with something stirring in your soul.

In the end, it's not all that important if you're belted into a $1.2 million Ferrari Enzo, a $50,000 supercharged Mustang, a Porsche Turbo, or a vintage Corvette Sting Ray. What matters is under your right foot, the sounds that fill the cockpit, and the fun of driving quickly.

Most everyone who loves fast cars remembers the first time they saw or heard an automobile that got their juices stirring. It might have been on television, in the parking lot of a racetrack, under your thumbs in a video game, or at an auto show.

Comedian and car expert Jay Leno recalls riding along on his bicycle as a kid and seeing a guy washing a Jaguar XK120. Now Leno has garages full of great automobiles.

I remember being driven into Elkhart Lake's Road America racetrack as Carroll Shelby, who was still racing then, roared by in a funny-looking, but fast, race car called *Ol' Yeller*. I was so taken by the scene that now, decades later, I'm at a computer still writing about quick machines.

My good friend and fellow automotive writer, Ken Gross, quit a perfectly good, high-level executive job to write about cars because of his fascination with great automobiles.

Mind you, it isn't all about power. Thumb through the pages of this book, and you'll find the great share of cars is beautiful and/or stirring to look at.

You might prefer the Ian Callum-inspired lines of an Aston Martin. The high-speed grace of a Pininfarina-clothed Ferrari. How Porsche manages to keep its machines looking both traditional and contemporary at the same time. Maybe it's the suit-of-armor look of the Bugatti Veyron. Or the way Saleen takes an everyday Mustang and makes it look like the mega-horsepower machine that it is.

Same thing inside the car, where it might be upholstered in the finest soft leathers and detailed with carbon fiber, or, as with the very quick cars from Lotus, the interior is done in a minimalist style with cloth seats and little trim, all to save weight and go faster.

It also isn't important how the car makes its horsepower. This might be the result of BMW engineering a 500-horsepower V-10 into the nose of a 5 Series sedan. The four turbochargers, 64 valves, and intriguing W-16 that pumps out 1,001 horsepower for Bugatti's Veyron 16.4. The tiny 1.8-liter four in a Lotus Elise. Or the pushrod, 2-valve-per-cylinder 505-horsepower V-8 in a Corvette Z06. What we care about is how fast it goes and how good it sounds.

The latter, by the way, isn't an accident. These days, automotive engineers spend a considerable amount of time making certain your favorite fast car sounds just right.

The good news is that modern electronic magic, like the ability of an automobile to sense when it is going out of control and, up to a point, put the car back on the straight and narrow, has taken some of the danger out of driving fast cars. It's spooky how well this works. Get into a right-hand turn too quickly, the front begins to understeer, and the system dials back the power and touches the right front brake just enough to bring the front end back in line.

The odd side to this is that some cars have become so powerful, and these safety systems so good, that it's difficult to take them to the limit on anything but a racetrack. Indy 500 winner Dario Franchitti loves his Ferrari F40 specifically because it isn't filled with these electronic aids and has to be driven with this firmly in mind.

All part of the fun of fast automobiles. So sit down, open the book, and start reading.

CHAPTER 1

THE CLASSICS

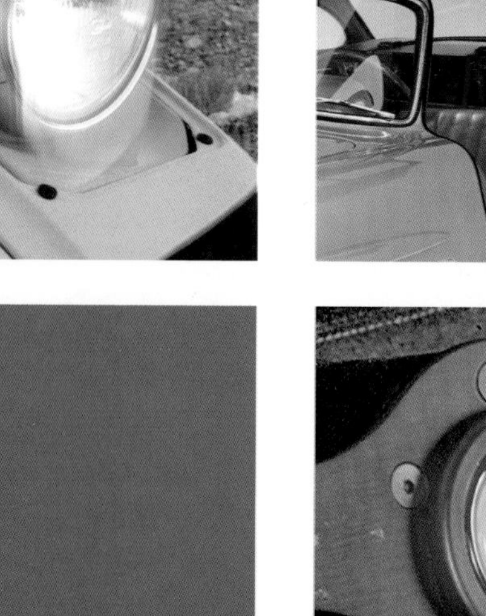

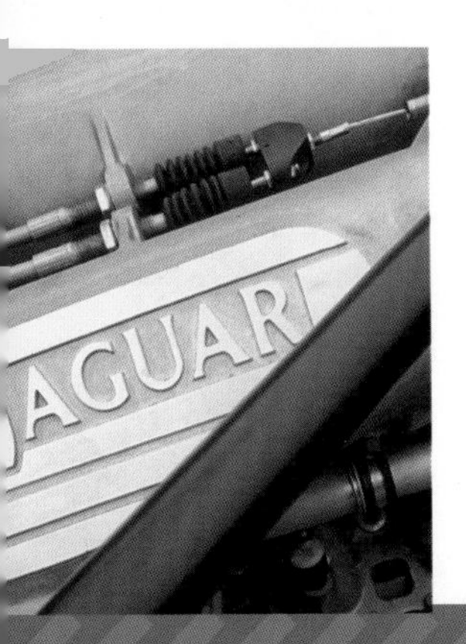

For all the hubbub about high-performance automobiles these days, supercars are not a new phenomenon. There has always been an inventor trying to build a faster automobile (make that a "horseless carriage"), or someone who tinkered with existing designs to make them quicker, or a mechanic who tried to get the performance of a twin from a single-cylinder engine.

We're not going back that far, but we need to pay homage to the great machines that led to modern supercars. Cars like the Alfa Romeo Carabo were the essential design studies leading to today's exotics. We have to include a few Corvettes, because what other automobile has offered the power-for-the-dollar of America's most famous sports car? The DeTomaso/Ford Pantera gets credit for bringing the exotic world into the hands of the more average guy, even if those hands were often grease stained keeping the car running.

Ferraris must be included because . . . well . . . a book about supercars must include Ferraris, as they represent the very nature of the famous Italian exotics.

Ford's GT40 may have found its fame on the racetrack, but there was also a street version. And that iconic body shape alone makes it an exotic car hall of fame candidate. Many Jaguar XJ220s may have ended up having their fate decided by the courts—an undeserved end for great cars—but that doesn't take away from the quality of the big cat's design.

Lamborghini's Miura and Countach were landmark machines in their era, prodding Ferrari to great things. Maserati's recent return to the exotic car world means we must pay our respects to the Bora.

To many traditional car fans, there is only one great exotic from the 1950s: the Mercedes-Benz 300SL. So it's a shoe-in to be included here. Just as certainly, many of the newest fans, those who have learned much about great cars from the Internet and video games, have earned a place here for the early Nissan Skylines. And, of course, you can't do a book about fast cars without including the name Shelby. These are automobiles you'll find in auctions, museums, and great car collections, the machines that paved the way for modern supercars.

BERTONE ALFA ROMEO CARABO

So what is this crazy-looking, green, 40-year-old, show car doing in a modern book about supercars? It is another of the benchmark automobiles included to give us perspective. There are still several major automotive designers who will point to the Carabo as a major inspiration for doing what they do today.

BERTONE ALFA ROMEO CARABO

Price: N/A
Engine: 230-horsepower, 2.0-liter V-6
0–60 mph: 6.4 seconds
Top speed: 155 mph

Designed for the 1968 Paris Motor Show, the Carabo was created at the famed Italian design house Bertone by Marcello Gandini, who later did such famous machines as the Lamborghini Countach, Lancia Stratos, and Bugatti EB110. This was an era when

designers were making a break from the traditional soft, curved styles to firm, hard edges. This is most notable in the transition from the Lamborghini Miura to the automaker's next model: the Countach.

"Louvers," said BMW's modern design guru Chris Bangle when discussing the Carabo. "What ever happened to louvers?" They were quite the design element around 1970, ending up on the rear body of everything from the Lamborghini Miura to the Ford Torino.

The straight lines and squares continued to the interior of the Carabo, which you enter through flip-up doors. Gandini would later use these on the Countach, and the doors have also been employed on such modern cars as the Ferrari Enzo, Mercedes-Benz SLR, and Saleen S7.

Did You Know?

Under the bodywork is the chassis of a well-known Alfa Romeo race car, the 33, which was powered by a small V-8. The show car is also known for its iridescent green color, that of a beetle that shares the name Carabo.

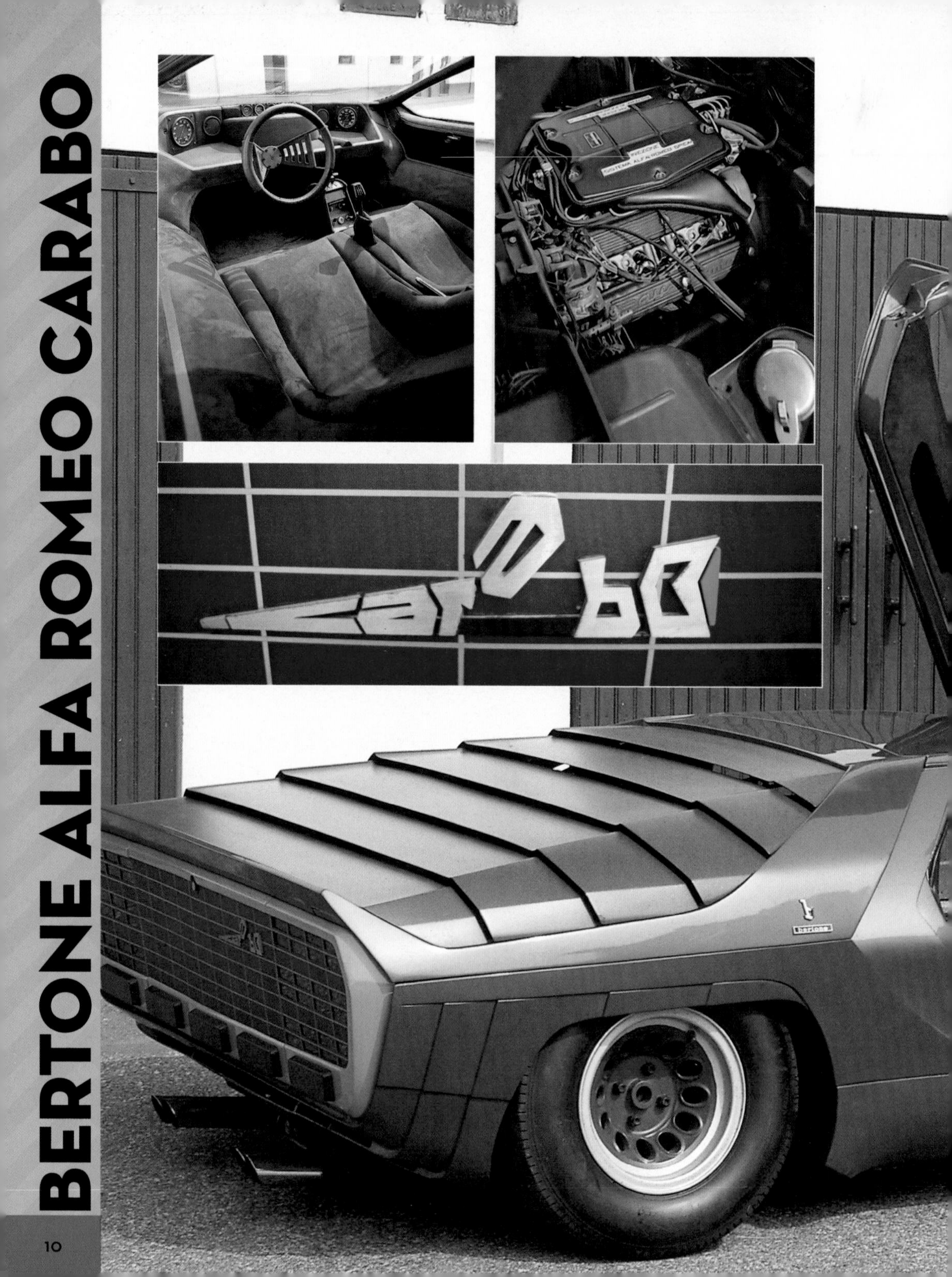

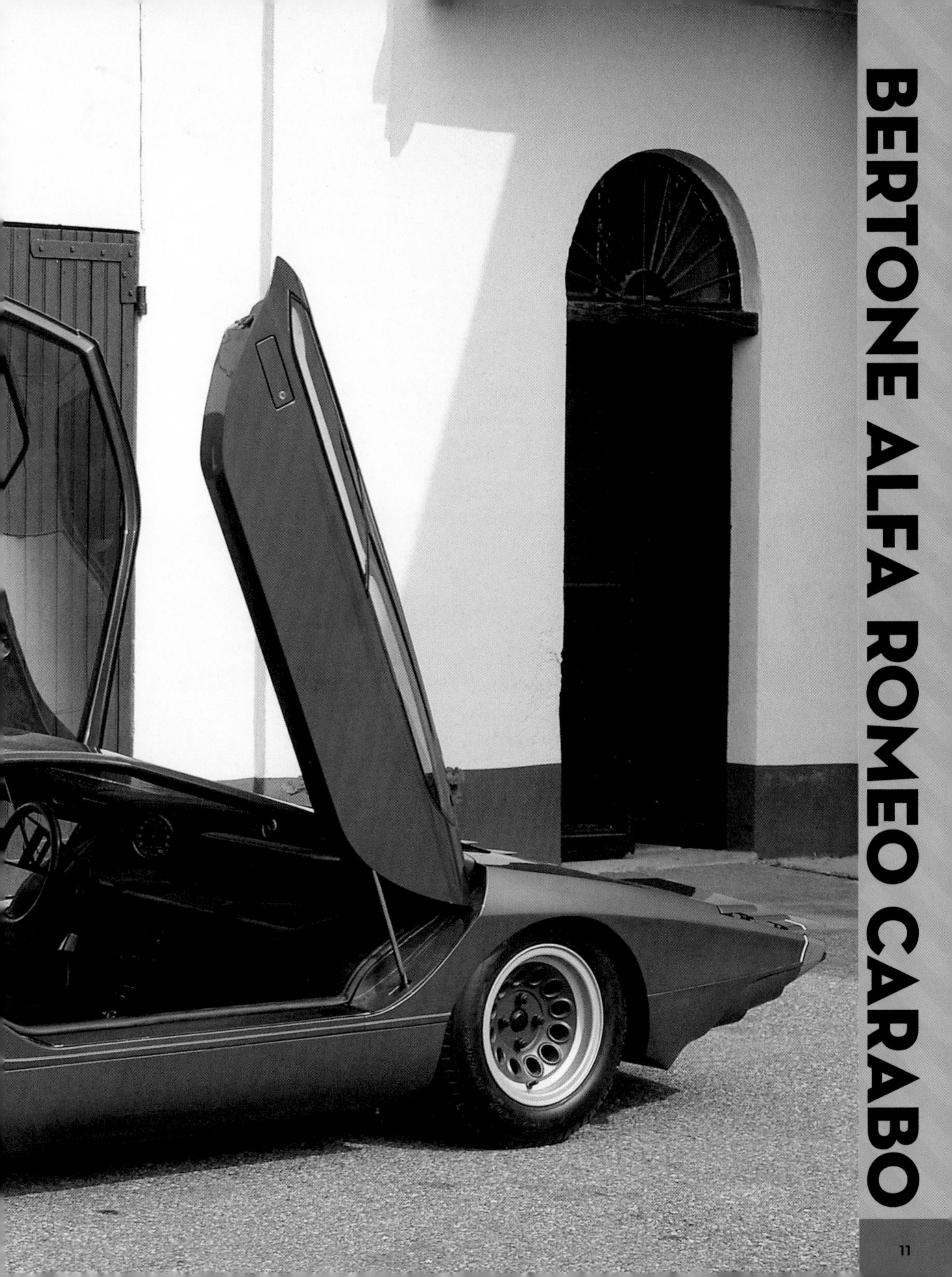

BERTONE ALFA ROMEO CARABO

BMW M1

BMW was hungry to beat its German rival, Porsche, on the racetrack and gave it a try with its front-engine CSi coupes. But that wasn't enough, so the Munich-based automaker decided to create its own mid-engine coupe to beat Porsche.

Called the M1, the engine was developed by BMW Motorsports. The exterior shape was assigned to famed Italian designer, Giorgetto Giugiaro. Chassis development went to Lamborghini. Both the chassis and fiberglass bodies were made in Italy but assembled in Germany.

BMW M1
Price: $60,000 (1981)
Engine: 277-horsepower, 3.5-liter inline six
0–60 mph: 5.3 seconds
Top speed: 162 mph

It was a nice try, but the project stretched out too long, and there were racing homologation problems. In the end, the M1 was raced most successfully in the U.S. IMSA series and by Grand Prix drivers in a one-marque series called Procar. Only 450 BMW M1s were built.

Ah, the rear window louvers of the M1, a feature of many performance cars in the 1970s. Under that lid is the BMW Motorsports straight six with its 277 horsepower and 243 lb-ft of torque. Aft of that is a ZF five-speed manual gearbox.

By today's standards, the cockpit of the M1 looks a bit sparse, but it's quite functional. The flat instrument panel has a no-nonsense display, while the seats are a bit flat but comfortable. And doesn't that steering wheel look naked without an air bag?

Did You Know?

BMW launched the M1 at the 1978 Paris Auto Show, where it was a sensation. Giorgetto Giugiaro's design shows hints of an earlier BMW supercar study, Paul Bracq's 1972 Turbo. The M1 can also be seen as an evolved, softer-edged design modeled after Giugiaro's well-known shapes for the Lotus Esprit and the DeLorean.

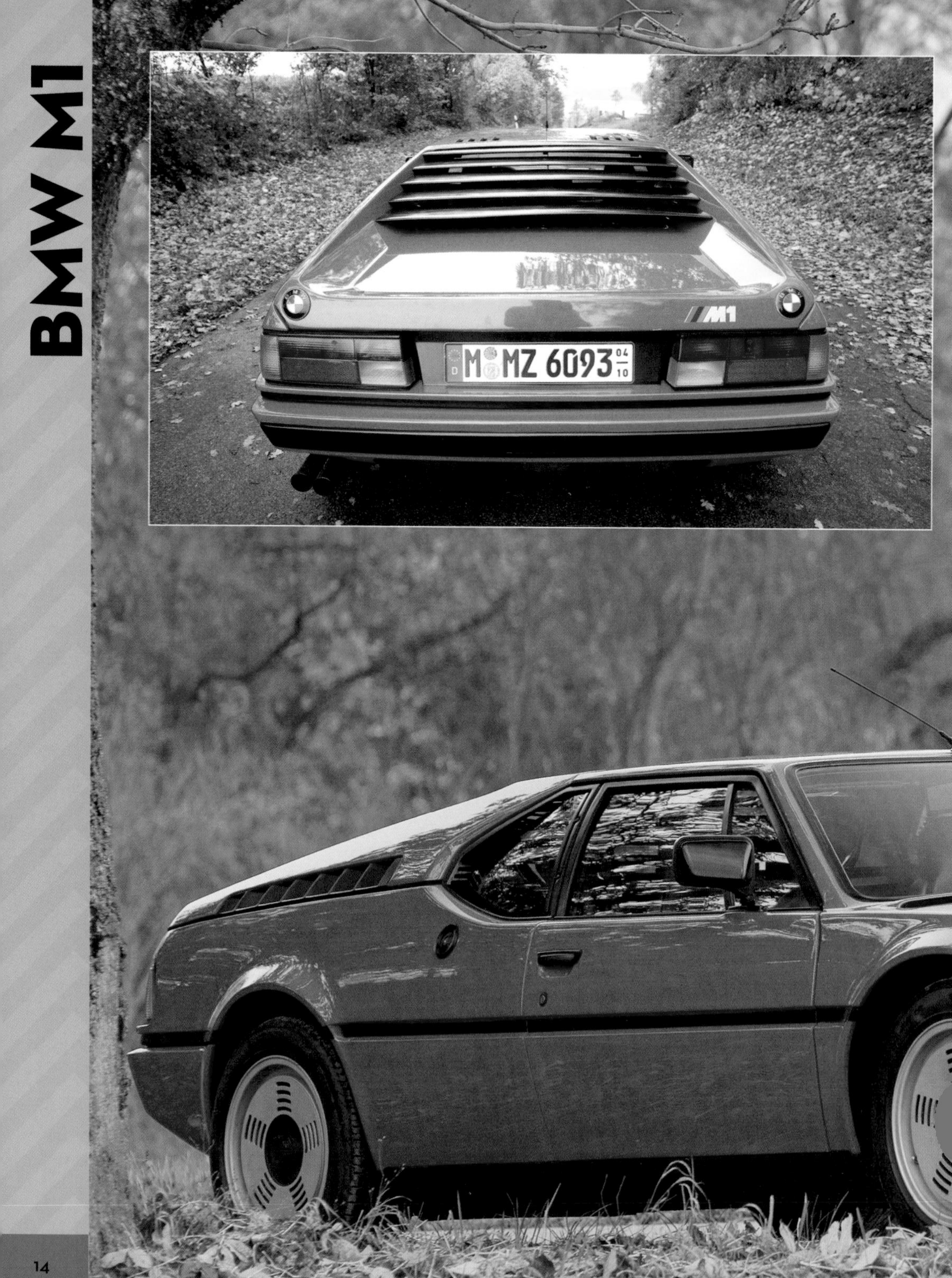
M1
M MZ 6093

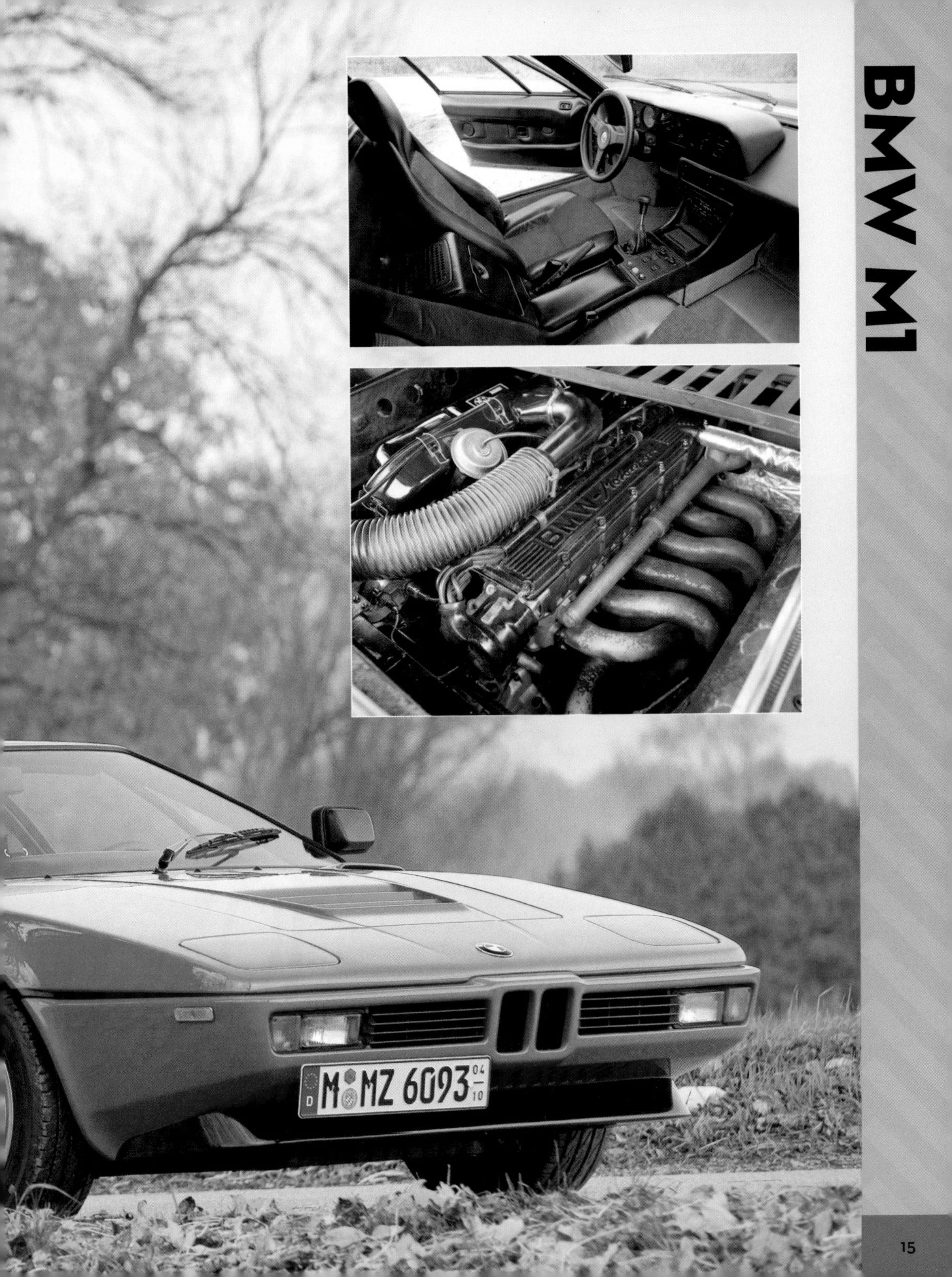
M MZ 6093

So what is an older Corvette doing in a modern book about supercars? Go back through the history of great sports cars, and ask yourself what other machine has provided more high-horsepower fun to more people than the Corvette?

Why the Sting Ray? It's symbolic of the great Corvettes, and to many it was the best 'Vette until the advent of the C5 in 1997. The landmark Sting Ray shape began with a drawing by young Peter Brock, who would later design the Shelby Cobra Daytona coupe. Zora Arkus-Duntov, godfather of the Corvette, had to work from Chevrolet's parts bin but nonetheless created a sports car that worked not just on the street but the racetrack as well.

There's something particularly exciting

CORVETTE STING RAY/ GRAND SPORT

Price: $4,295 plus options (1966)

Engine: 425-horsepower, 7.0-liter V-8 (optional)

0–60 mph: 4.8 seconds

Top speed: 140 mph

about the Sting Ray interior with its half-circle shapes ahead of driver and passenger. Big gauges make for easy reading. That steering wheel rim feels a bit thin by modern standards, but it's great fun to be rowing through the four-speed manual gearbox as the small-block howls.

In 1962, Zora Arkus-Duntov was concerned over Ford's involvement with Carroll Shelby's Cobra program and designed the lightweight Grand Sport Corvette race car to fight it. GM management shut down the program and only five were built, making them the most treasured of all Corvettes. The best Grand Sport engine was a 377-cubic-inch V-8 with 550 horsepower.

Did You Know?

Sting Rays could be had with Chevrolet small- or (as of 1965) big-block V-8s. On the next page, you'll see the fuel-injected version at 375 horsepower, though by 1965, the list included five versions of the small-block and the 425-horsepower 396-cubic-inch big-block V-8.

293 GI
QVU 08

CORVETTE ZR1

In the late 1980s, Chevrolet was looking to bolster the Corvette's reputation. The world's biggest automaker had recently bought one of the world's smallest, Lotus. The little English firm was as famous for its engineering prowess as its automobiles, so Chevrolet asked it to rework the 5.7-liter L98 small-block V-8 to make the 'Vette among the fastest sports cars in the world.

Lotus had to retain several dimensions, like the distance between cylinder bore centers and the basic size. Formula 1 guru Tony Rudd was put on the project and designed a dual-overhead-cam V-8 with a number of advanced components, 375 horsepower, and 370 lb-ft of torque.

It certainly bumped the ZR1 well up the acceleration list with a 0–60 time of less than five seconds in 1990 and a top speed above 180 mph.

Lotus' redesign of Chevrolet's small-block V-8 is both powerful and pretty. Sixteen intake runners feed four valves per cylinder for those 375 horses. ZR1 V-8s were built by Mercury Marine, which was skilled at producing high-performance engines, and shipped to Bowling Green, Kentucky, for installation in the 'Vettes.

For all its qualities, the ZR1 was not a big success. It cost about twice that of a normal C4. Externally the only major difference, other than badging, was a unique tail. But come 1991, the C4 got the same tail, and there was little difference in the two cars' interiors. Chevy shot itself in the foot with the ZR1.

CORVETTE ZR1
Price: $58,995 (1990)
Engine: 375-horsepower, 5.7-liter V-8
0–60 mph: 4.6 seconds
Top speed: 180 mph

Did You Know?

In addition to designing the engine of the ZR1, Lotus helped develop the suspension so that it would be able to handle the extra power. And it did, with the super 'Vette gaining a reputation as the best-handling sports car in the United States and among the best in the world.

DE TOMASO PANTERA

It's said that Elvis Presley shot his Pantera.

This was in the early 1970s, when the automotive world was going through a transition to mid-engine placement for exotic cars. Of the Detroit automakers, only Ford built a mid-engine exotic, outsourcing production of its Pantera to Alessandro De Tomaso in Italy.

Priced "around $10,000" when new, the mid-engine Ford provided great performance for the money, thanks to its 5.7-liter Ford V-8. But the Italian cars were plagued with problems, the most famous being rust, though there were various mechanical bugs—which is why Elvis put a bullet in his when it wouldn't start.

Today, specialists can easily fix all the bugaboos and, at $50,000–$60,000 for very nice examples, Panteras again provide great performance for the money.

DE TOMASO PANTERA

Price: "Around $10,000" (1971)
Engine: 310-horsepower, 5.7-liter V-8
0–60 mph: 5.5 seconds
Top speed: 129 mph

The interior of the Pantera is a classic layout for the period, gauges angled toward the driver. The tall shifter in its gate looks great but didn't always give you the promised gear.

Technically, the Pantera had the right stuff: mid-engine layout, four-wheel disc brakes, rack and pinion steering, and its famous Goodyear Arriva tires. In its first year, before major emissions equipment sapped power, a Pantera would leap to 60 mph in 5.5 seconds, a good time for the era.

Did You Know?

American Tom Tjarda designed the Pantera while working for Ghia in Italy. Panteras were built from 1971 until the early 1990s, though importation to the United States ended in 1975. Through the years, the basic shape never changed, though Panteras grew ever-larger fender flares and spoilers.

FERRARI 365 GTB/4 DAYTONA

It seems difficult to believe now, but in the late 1960s, the now-beloved Ferrari 275 GTB/4 wasn't a hot seller. A young designer at Pininfarina, Leonardo Fioravanti, took it upon himself to design a new body for the chassis of the GTB.

Enzo Ferrari liked the design, and Ferrari presented the new road car with a stunning shape at the 1968 Paris Auto Show: the 365 GTB/4. Because Ferrari 330/P4 race cars had finished 1-2-3 at the Daytona International Speedway in January 1968, the new GTB/4 got the nickname "Daytona," and it stuck forever.

Last of the great front-engine Ferrari road cars until the 1996 550 Maranello, the Daytona—built as a coupe and roadster—is a legend in its own right.

FERRARI 365 GTB/4 DAYTONA

Price: $19,500 (when new)
Engine: 405-horsepower, 4.4-liter V-12
0–60 mph: 5.9 seconds
Top speed: 173 mph

Classic stuff in a Ferrari: the 4.4-liter, 60-degree V-12 with a bank of six Weber carburetors down its middle. Rated at 405 horsepower, the engine makes an epic sound, especially in the last 1,000 rpm before its 6,800-rpm redline. Its gearbox is a rear-mounted five-speed.

Ferrari instrument panels have often been considered the best in the business, and the Daytona's is a classic. All gauges are white-on-black, dominated by the tachometer and speedometer. Cars weren't as reliable then as now, so the smaller gas gauge and clock are joined by dials for coolant and oil temperature, oil pressure, and amps.

Did You Know?

With his design of the Daytona, Fioravanti wanted to make a break from the traditional Ferrari rounder shapes and did so with the 365 GTB/4. Although originally sold for around $20,000, a nice Daytona convertible would sell for $500,000 and up today.

FERRARI 365 GTB/4 DAYTONA

FERRARI 365 GTB/4 DAYTONA

FERRARI 365 GTB/4 BERLINETTA BOXER

In the early 1970s, the trend among exotic cars was toward a mid-engine design. Enzo Ferrari was a conservative when it came to some technical matters and was slow to go to the new layout, but Lamborghini forced his hand with the Miura and Countach. While critics chided Ferrari for being behind the times, the factory at Maranello was tackling the problem.

Ferrari's mid-engine answer went into production in 1973 and was called the 365 GTB/4 Berlinetta Boxer, though it's usually simply referred to as "The Boxer." Once again, Pininfarina sculpted the body for Ferrari. The form was based on a show car called the P6 and, as with the Daytona, it was penned by Leonardo Fioravanti. Though not as dramatic looking as the Countach, The Boxer is ultimately a more beautiful design.

FERRARI 365 GTB/4 BERLINETTA BOXER

Price: $85,000 (512BB certified for U.S. sale)
Engine: 360-horsepower, 5.0-liter flat 12
0–60 mph: 5.1 seconds
Top speed: est. 188 mph

Ferrari was known for its V-12 engines but didn't like that solution when it came to placing the powerplant low behind the cockpit. So engineers basically folded the V-12's cylinder banks out until they had a flat 12. In original 4.4-liter form, it had 344 horsepower, the 5.0-liter 512BB boasting 360, its injected, low-emissions form having 340.

With the mid-engine placement, the exotic cars became rather wide with broad passenger compartments, making them more difficult to enter. Unlike today's highly bolstered seats, Boxers' seats are rather flat. Between the seats is a typical (great-looking) Ferrari shift gate.

Did You Know?
Early Ferrari Boxers weren't officially imported into the United States but were sold on the "gray market" and certified by aftermarket companies. During the late 1970s and 1980s, the government took great interest in the exotic car market, and several of the more interesting supercars were not sold in the States.

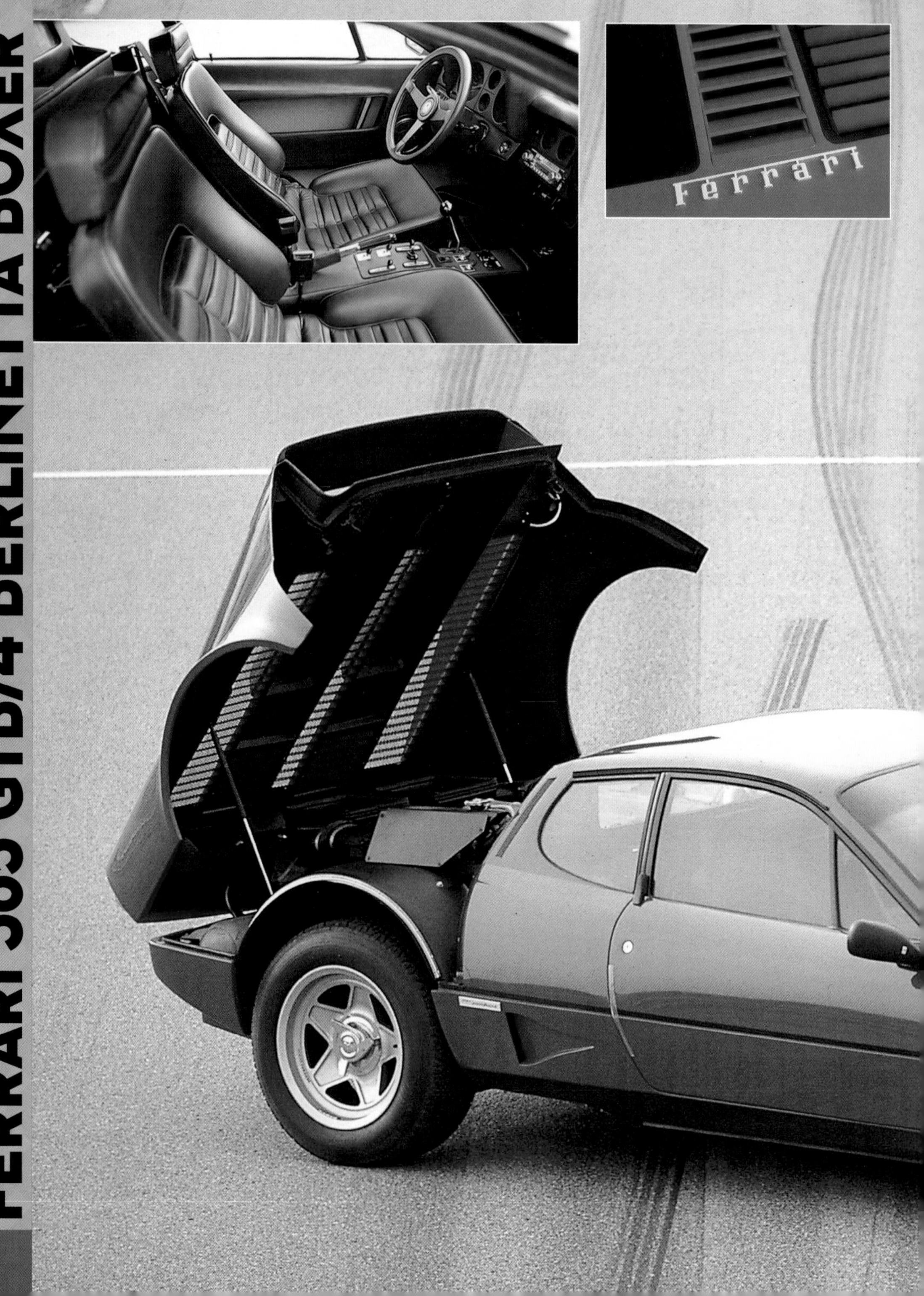
Ferrari

FERRARI F40

Some automakers would celebrate a 40th anniversary with a dinner and maybe a new trim package for one car model, but not Ferrari. It created an entire automobile. Come July 1987, coinciding with the 40th anniversary, Enzo Ferrari personally presented the F40 to the public.

Pininfarina penned the bodywork for the new mid-engine Ferrari, which had a twin-turbo V-8 under the rear deck. Thanks to 478 horsepower, the lightweight Ferrari was able to clock just 3.8 seconds to 60 mph, and if you kept the pedal down—and the road was straight—it would continue to 201 mph.

It looks like one very slick Pininfarina-sculpted street machine from the outside, but under the carbon fiber, the F40 shows its race car heritage. Suspensions have unequal-length A-arms, coil springs, Koni shocks, and adjustable ride height, the F40 lowering itself at higher speeds for better aerodynamics.

FERRARI F40

Price: $415,000
Engine: 478-horsepower, 2.9-liter twin-turbo V-8
0–60 mph: 3.8 seconds
Top speed: 201 mph

Look through the plastic rear window of the F40, and you'll see the 478-horsepower V-8. Engineers equipped the 2.9-liter powerplant with a pair of IHI turbochargers and intercoolers. Torque is an impressive 425 lb-ft. The four-speed manual transmission could be had with or without synchromesh.

You could outfit your F40 from road to track purposes. Inside were the options of three seat designs of ever-greater sportiness, the driver needing a custom fitting. Even air conditioning and roll-up windows were on the options list.

Did You Know?

Ferrari's F40 benefited from coming along in the early days of carbon fiber use in production cars. As a result, the huge rear engine cover weighs a mere 48.5 pounds, with wing. In total, the F40 weighs just 2,420 pounds.

FERRARI F50

Ferrari's 50th anniversary gift to the automotive world was the F50. Built between 1995 and 1997, it was another example—like the F40 and Enzo—of Ferrari showing the best it could create.

This time, Ferrari said it wanted to build a two-seat Formula 1 car for the street. So it began with the V-12 used in a previous Formula 1 car and developed it to 4.7 liters. The engine basics were also used in Ferrari's 333SP race car.

The chassis is an F1-style tub made of carbon fiber, while the suspension designs also reflect racing thinking. Around all this went Pininfarina bodywork that also leaned on F1 technology, being made of carbon fiber, Kevlar, and Nomex.

That's a lot of stuff back there, very unlike today's neat and tidy engine compartments. Let's see, there's the 4.7-liter, 513-horsepower V-12 with its carbon-fiber air box, twisted headers, and big catalytic converters; the six-speed manual transmission; and then the pushrod-actuated coil spring/tube shock assemblies.

Pininfarina's design of the F50 looks rather like a flowing version of the F40 design. Not surprisingly, the F50 was fine-tuned in Pininfarina's wind tunnel, leading to the rear wing, a smooth underbody, and those large air ducts in the nose that not only vent hot air but also add downforce.

F50s have a removable hardtop, but no place to store it. So the driver has to leave it at home. And unlike the Formula 1 theme in the rest of the car, the interior has nicely upholstered seats, power windows, and even air conditioning.

FERRARI F50

Price: $480,000
Engine: 513-horsepower, 4.7-liter V-12
0–60 mph: 3.6 seconds
Top speed: 203 mph

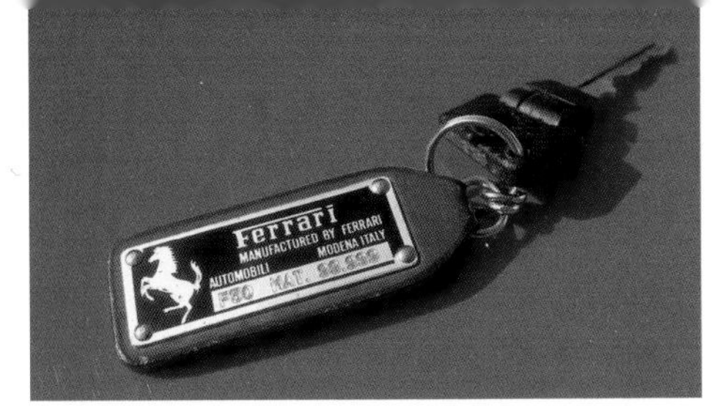

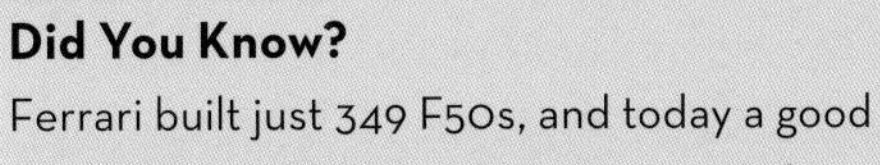

Did You Know?

Ferrari built just 349 F50s, and today a good example is worth about twice its original $480,000 tag.

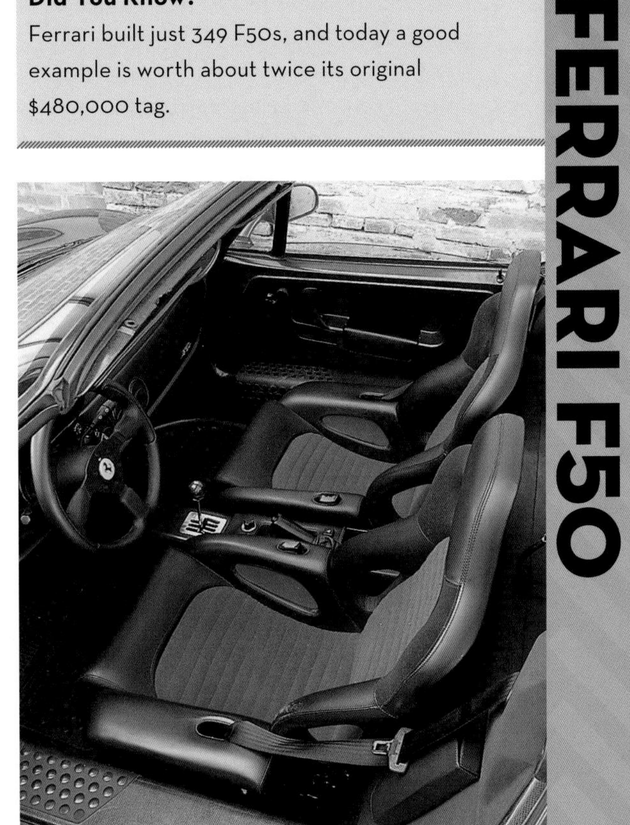

FORD GT40

When Henry Ford II wasn't able to buy Ferrari, he set off to build his own car to beat the Italian automaker. His team, which included Carroll Shelby, started off a bit slow but ended up winning the crown jewel of sports car racing, the 24 Hours of Le Mans, in 1966, 1967, 1968, and 1969.

They did it with the mid-engine Ford GT40, which came in a variety of forms including the Mark I, II, and IV race cars, and the Mark III road car. What you see here is a Mark I race car being used for the street.

Not only was the GT40 (so named for being 40 inches tall) a success on the track, but the Ford became one of the hallmark performance cars of the second half of the twentieth century ... and spawned the modern Ford GT exotic car.

The stuff of kids' dreams, getting behind the wheel with its FORD GT logo. Being a race car, there's no speedometer, just the big tach and dials to check oil, fuel, coolant, and electrical functions. Simple switches for lights, fans, etc., plus one concession to the times: a cigarette lighter.

Although big-block Ford V-8s were used for the Mark II and IV GTs, the Is and IIIs had 4.7-liter V-8s. The smaller pushrod engines were tuned to 380 horsepower and 330 lb-ft of torque for the race versions, while the road machines had 306 horsepower and 329 lb-ft of torque. The small-block GT40s all had five-speed manual gearboxes.

FORD GT40

Price: $18,500 (MkIII when new)
Engine: 306-horsepower, 4.7-liter V-8 (road version)
0–60 mph: est. 6.2 seconds
Top speed: est. 164 mph (depending on gearing)

Did You Know?

Some would argue this is the most memorable car shape since World War II. The original inspiration for the GT40 was the Lola GT, and the Fords were built with a semi-monocoque chassis, upper A-arm and lower trailing-arm suspensions, and disc brakes.

JAGUAR XJ220

Like many automakers, Jaguar got caught up in the mid-engine exotic craze of the late 1980s. Its contribution was the XJ220, which was developed by Tom Walkinshaw Racing. Originally meant to have a V-12 engine, the XJ220 ended up with a twin-turbo V-6 and all-wheel drive.

There was a great deal of aluminum used in the chassis and body of the beautiful Jag, which got its name from its proposed top speed: 220 mph.

JAGUAR XJ220

Price: $580,000 (1992)
Engine: 542-horsepower, 3.5-liter twin-turbo V-6
0–60 mph: 3.8 seconds
Top speed: 220 mph

Unfortunately, the XJ220 was a victim of bad timing. A collapse in the exotic automotive market caused all values to drop, and many prospective XJ220 owners walked

away from their deposits. Lawsuits were begun, court battles followed, and the XJ220 was the victim. Sad, as it's a great car.

Jaguar designer Keith Helfet gets credit for the XJ220's beautiful exterior design. Not only is it good looking, but the shape is a natural compared to such Jaguar classics as the D-Type in the background.

Judged against most supercars, the XJ220's interior is like a limousine's. The seats are supportive for hard driving but also downright comfy. Layout and execution of the dashboard makes it obvious this is the product of a luxury automaker . . . its 220-mph potential aside.

Did You Know?

If there was a fly in the XJ220's soup, it was the engine. When the 6.2-liter V-12 was dropped from the project, it was replaced by a twin-turbo V-6, the first in Jaguar's history. At 542 horsepower, power isn't the problem, but the engine sounds like it belongs to a very fast tractor.

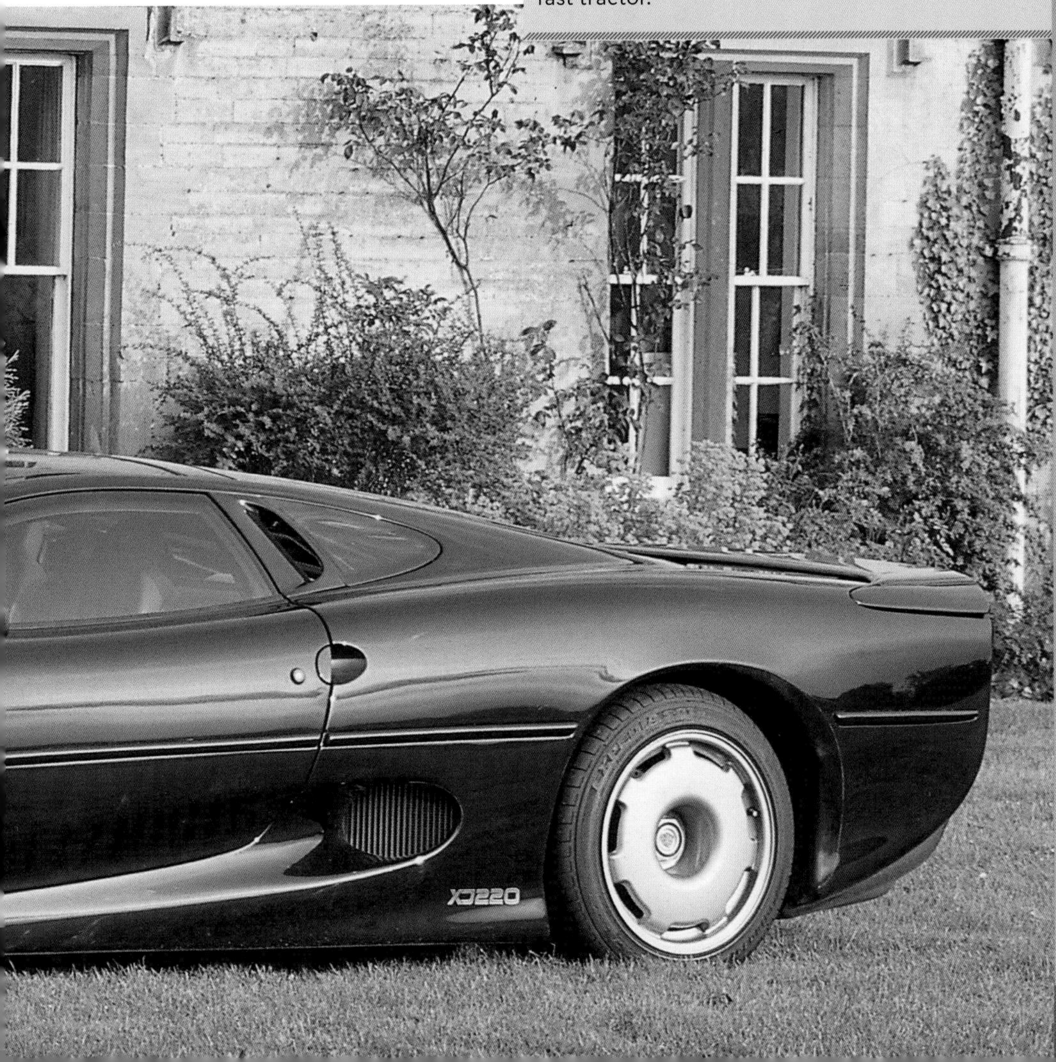

JAGUAR

XJ220
JAGUAR
XJ220

LAMBORGHINI MIURA

It was the sensation of the 1966 Geneva Auto Show and still turns heads today.

Lamborghini had decided to challenge the exotic car world by applying the mid-engine movement, which had taken over the racing car world, to a street machine. The previous autumn, it had presented the chassis with its boxed central frame, A-arm suspensions, and—this was the treat—the company's V-12 engine arranged sideways at the back.

Obviously, this chassis needed a special body, and Lamborghini went to Bertone, which produced the wonderfully low-slung shape of what would be called the Miura. Comedian and Miura owner Jay Leno remembers when the Miura was new: "I remember seeing a picture in one of the (car) magazines of a Miura on Sunset Boulevard . . . and thinking, 'Geez, what

LAMBORGHINI MIURA

Price: $19,900 (1968)

Engine: 350-horsepower, 3.9-liter V-12

0–60 mph: 6.6 seconds

Top speed: 174 mph

is that?'"

Inside, a Miura is as much a statement about 1960s design and flow as it is about sport and ergonomics. But isn't it beautiful? You should hear the crisp snap as you shift gears through that metal shiftgate.

In the Miura's day, *Road & Track* magazine road tested the Lamborghini and called it "the most glamorous, exciting, and prestigious car in the world . . . it has its faults, but every enthusiast should have at least one Miura."

Did You Know?

Just one of the Miura's design quirks was to arrange the 60-degree, V-12 side-to-side aft of the cockpit. At 350 horsepower, the engine would get the Miura to 60 mph in just over 6.0 seconds, though later, more powerful versions would cut that to around the mid-5s.

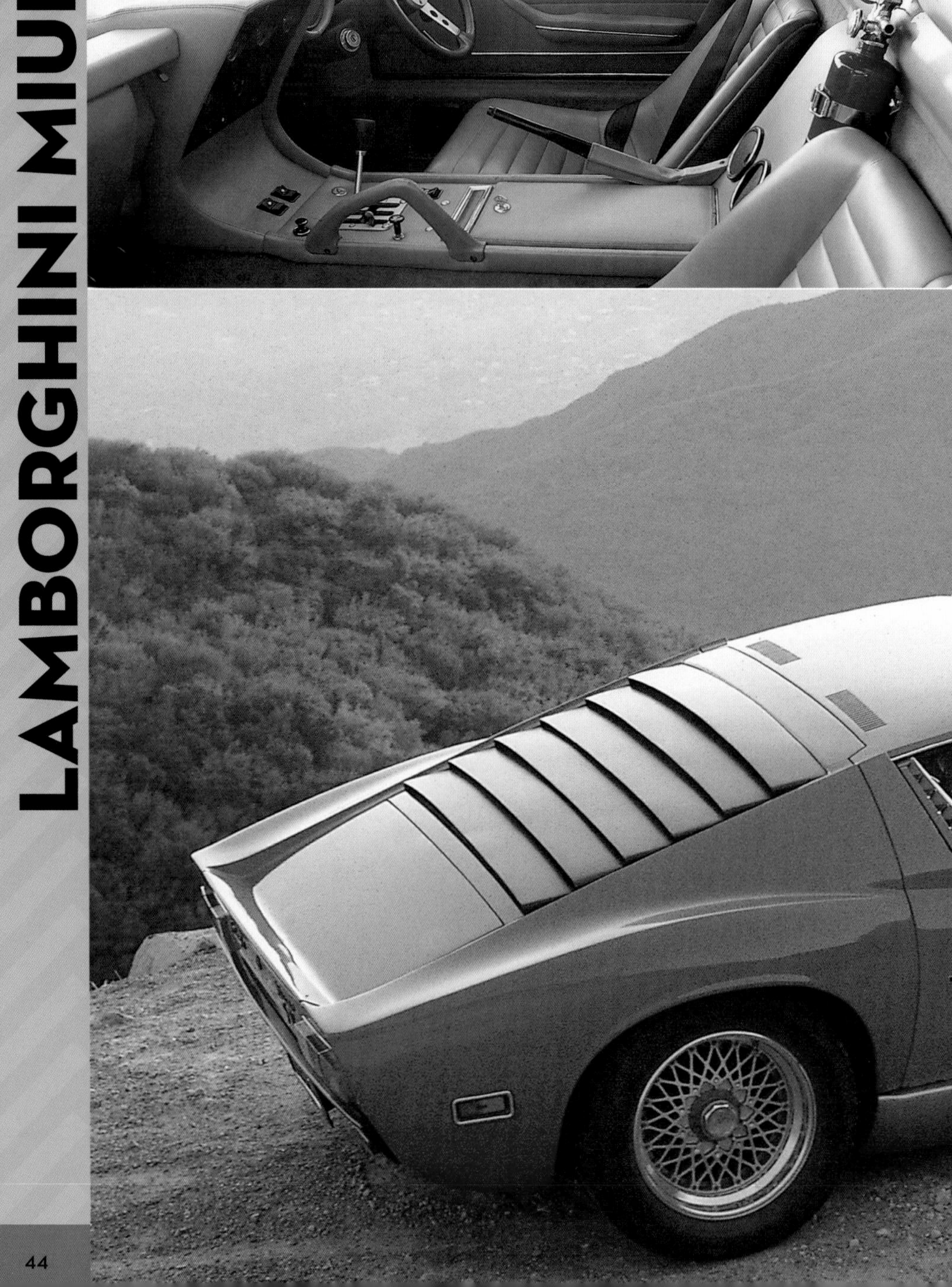

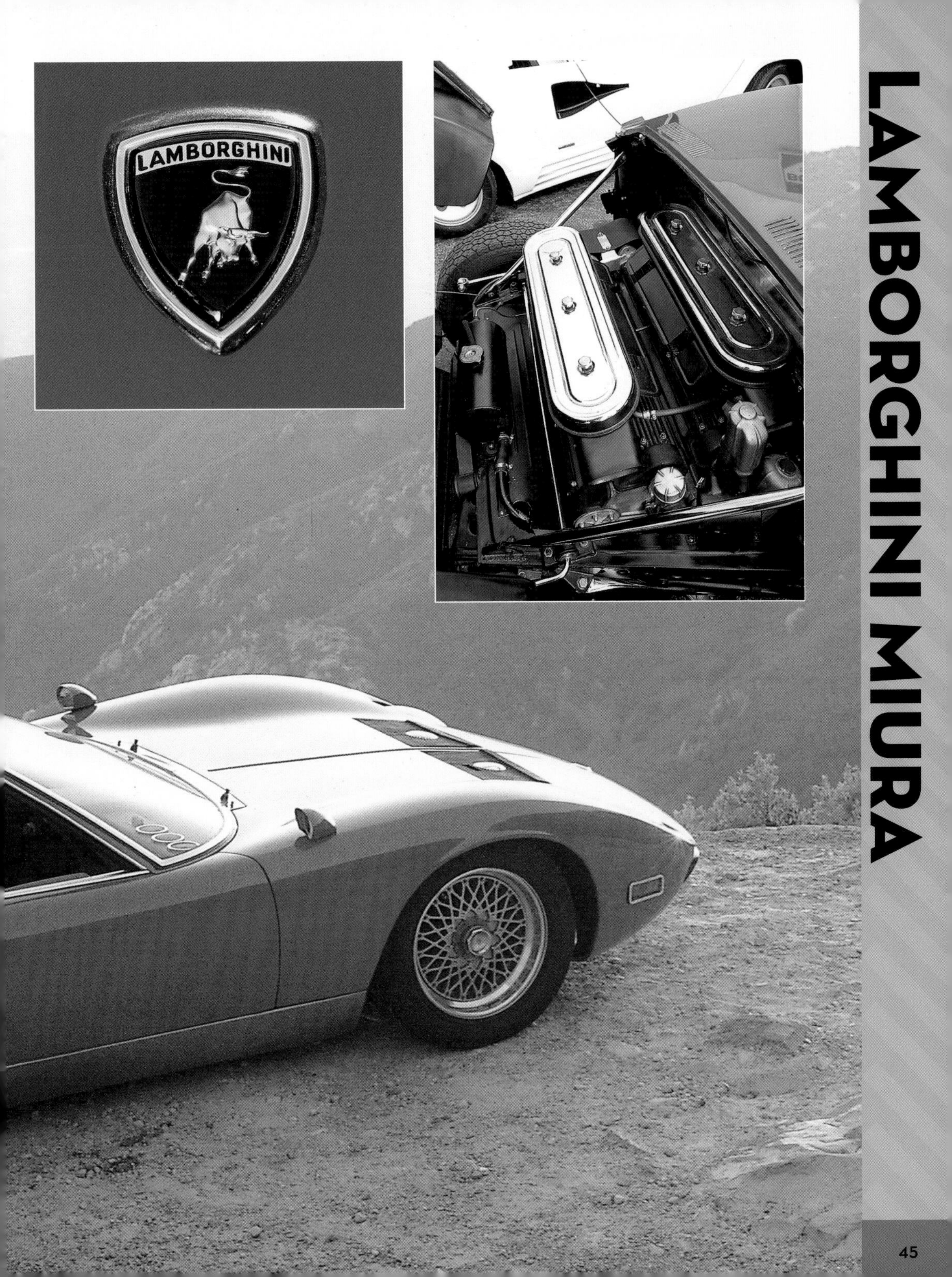
LAMBORGHINI

If you did a worldwide survey of the most recognizable automobile ever, there's a good chance Lamborghini's Countach would win. It's amazing . . . jaw dropping . . . stunning. Not necessarily beautiful, but eminently memorable.

Even its name, Countach, is the equivalent of saying "wow" when seeing a beautiful woman.

Marcello Gandini of Bertone was given the task to create the successor to the low, smooth, curvy, small Miura. The young designer went the opposite direction with flat surfaces and sharp lines. And then Bertone fitted the big supercar with those

LAMBORGHINI COUNTACH

Price: $85,000 (LP400S in 1979)
Engine: 353-horsepower, 3.9-liter V-12
0–60 mph: 5.8 seconds
Top speed: 180 mph

amazing front-hinged, flip-up doors.

That shape was formed in aluminum panels that were fixed to a steel frame. Inside all that was a big V-12 engine, slung in nose-to-tail, with the transmission forward under a cover in the interior.

So you raise the door and kind of ease yourself over the wide side sills and slip into those contoured seats. Next to you is the large center console that was needed to cover the big backwards transmission that sticks forward into the compartment.

This view is so 1970s: The steering wheel with no air bag. The row of gauges in the squared off, mouse-fur-covered instrument panel. The row of large warning lights. Now imagine the view through the steering wheel as the speedometer tops 175 mph.

Did You Know?

Under that rear cover is a large-block Lamborghini V-12 that had a displacement of 3.9 liters in the early Countachs. Over the years, the displacement went to 5.0 liters and then to 5.2 liters and with four valves per cylinder.

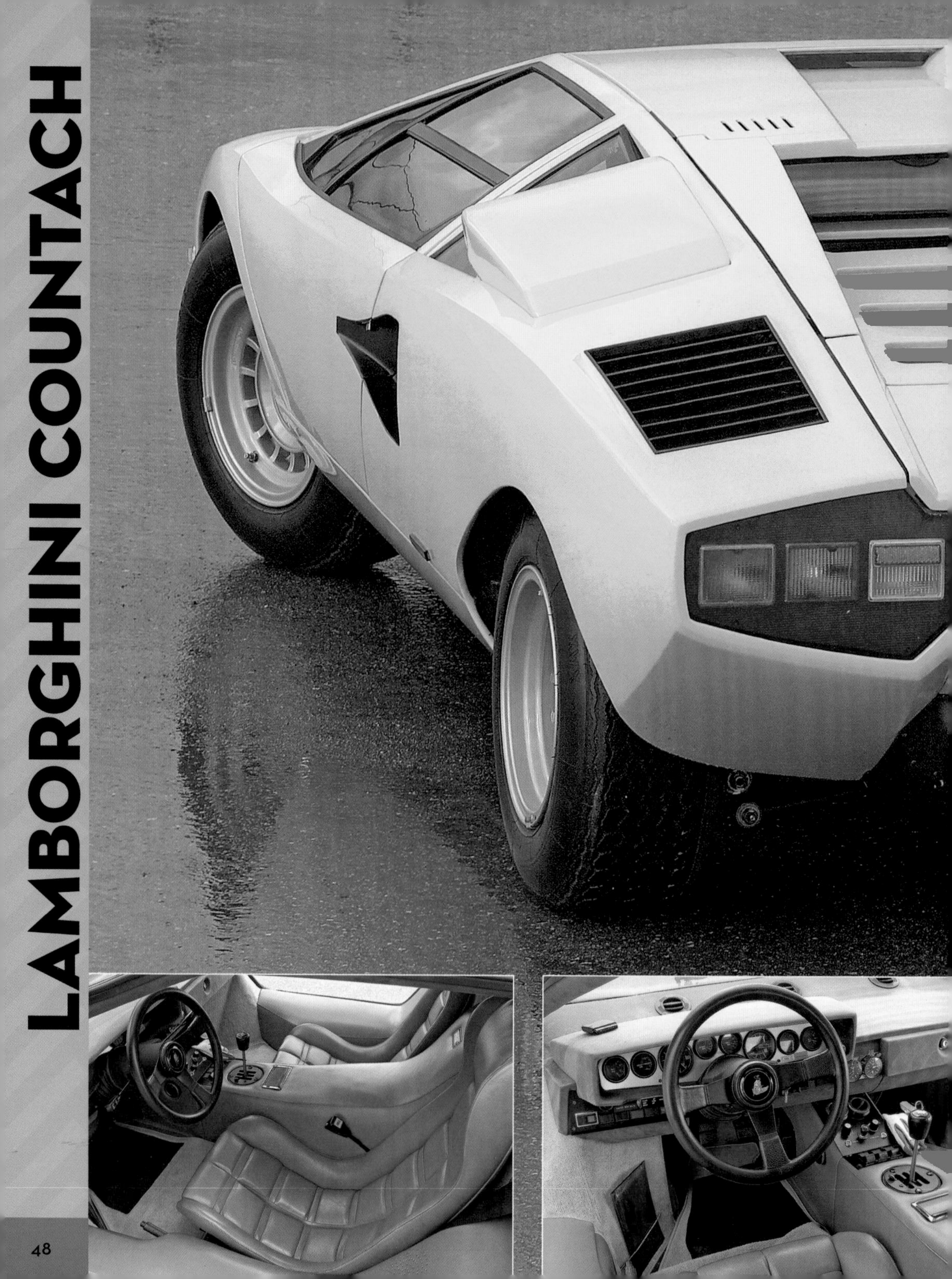

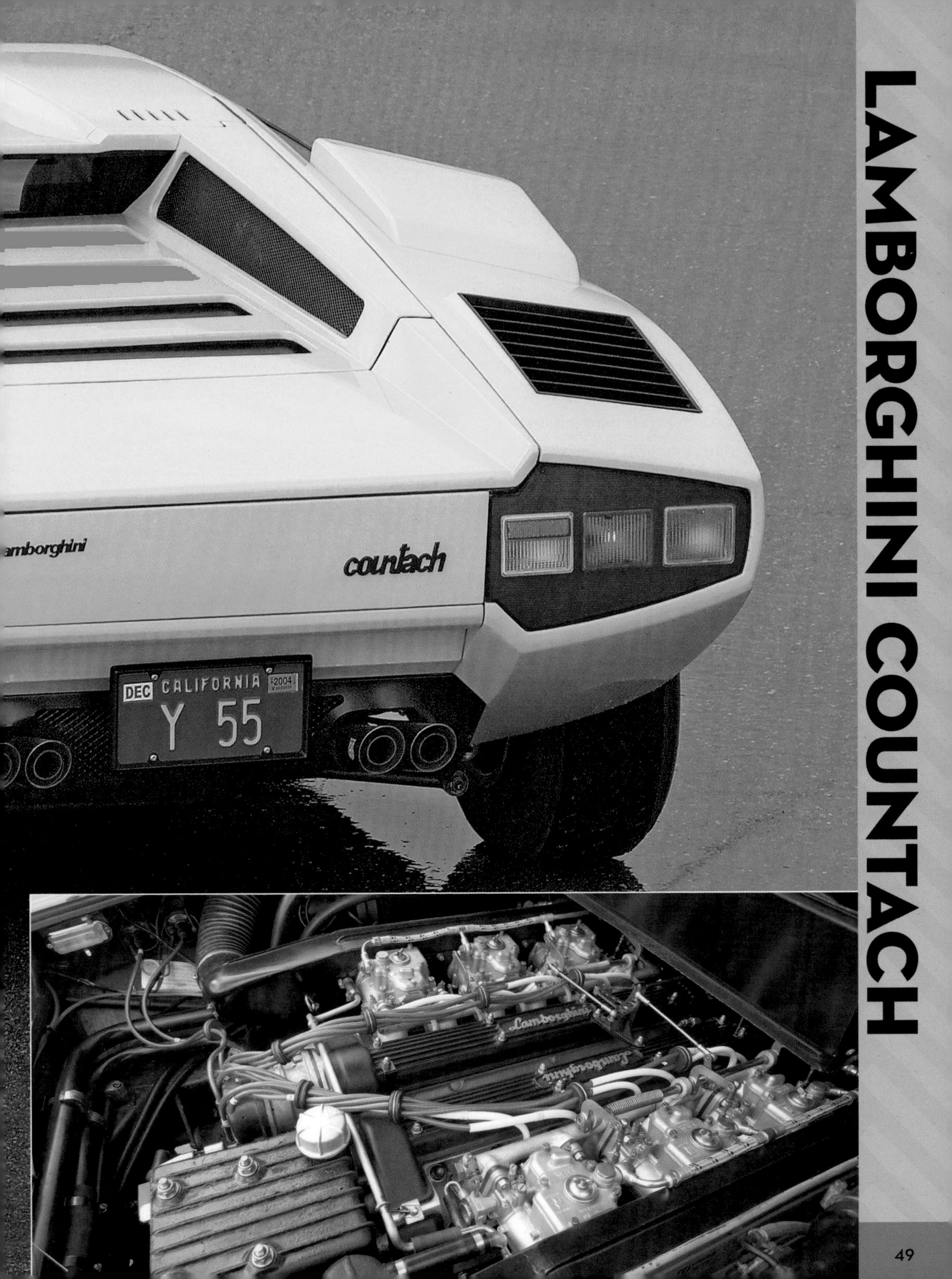
Lamborghini
countach
DEC CALIFORNIA 2004
Y 55
Lamborghini
Lamborghini

MASERATI BORA

Building a mid-engine exotic car was considered important for automakers in the early 1970s, so when the French automaker Citroën bought the Italian specialist firm Maserati, it decided to do the same. Being conservative, the owner didn't want anything as outrageous as the Countach and hired Giorgetto Giugiaro to draw a non-too-bold supercar. He did, and the result, while not as stirring as the Countach or Ferrari Boxer, is a very handsome machine, right up to its brushed stainless-steel roof.

Maserati's V-8 in the Bora has a long, storied history having once powered the automaker's race-winning sports cars. For the Bora, the engine was initially built with 4.7 liters and 310 horsepower, then opened up to 4.9 liters but got only 300 horsepower to meet U.S. emissions rules.

Under that large rear engine cover is the V-8 that is well insulated for noise from the passenger compartment. The seats are almost like lounge chairs, and driving the big V-8–powered machine is fun and surprisingly effortless.

MASERATI BORA

Price: $45,000 (1978)
Engine: 300-horsepower, 4.9-liter V-8
0–60 mph: 7.2 seconds
Top speed: 163 mph

Did You Know?

You can see hints of another Giugiaro Maserati, the front-engine Ghibli, in the Bora, which has a little brother, the similar-looking V-6-powered Merak. Built from 1971 until 1980, a good Bora can be had for $40,000 today.

MERCEDES-BENZ 300SL

One of the most iconic exotic cars of the 1950s was the Mercedes-Benz 300SL. Born from a successful racing program and developed under the guidance of the legendary engineer Rudolf Uhlenhaut, the SL put Mercedes on the map in what would become its most profitable market: the United States.

The name 300SL came from the car's 3.0-liter engine and SL for *Sport Leicht*, or Sport Light in German.

What makes the car so unique are its gullwing doors that pivot up from the center of the roof. It was the high-sided tube frame of the SL that necessitated the doors, and they made getting in and out difficult—pity women in skirts trying the maneuver—but forever stamped the image of the SL in the public's mind.

MERCEDES-BENZ 300SL

Price: $7,295 (1956)
Engine: 240-horsepower (SAE), 3.0-liter inline six
0–60 mph: 8.8 seconds
Top speed: 135 mph

Ultimately, the doors proved impractical, and a more conventional roadster succeeded the coupe.

Mercedes then, as now, was well-known for its engines. In the 300SL's case, this is a 3.0-liter straight six with port fuel injection. Angled 50 degrees to the left to allow for a low hood line, the engine has 240 (SAE) horsepower and 206 lb-ft of torque with a four-speed manual transmission.

Gullwing SLs often had plaid fabric upholstery, and to help the driver sneak in over the doorsill, the steering wheel would pivot upward. The interior of the later SL roadster had vertical stitching on the seats and round gauges flanking the vertical display (next page).

Did You Know?

Say "Mercedes-Benz 300SL" and the next word is inevitably "gullwing," but there was also a roadster version of the 300SL. More practical, thanks to a chassis redesign that allowed conventional doors, the roadster was produced from 1958 until 1963 and updated with such equipment as disc brakes.

MERCEDES-BENZ 300SL

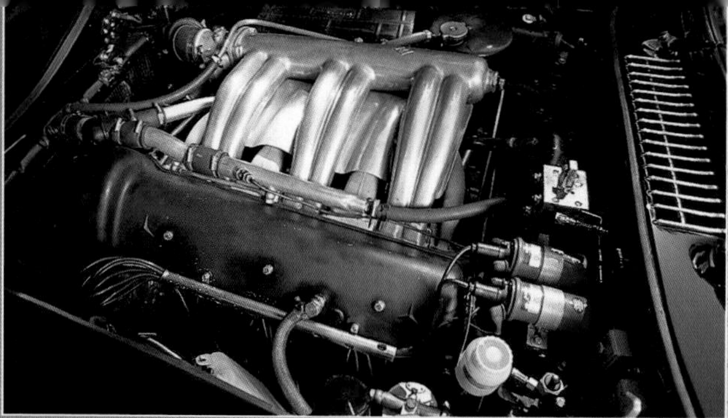

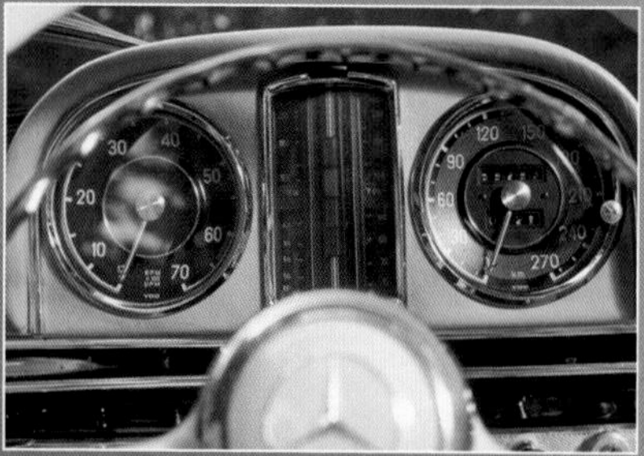

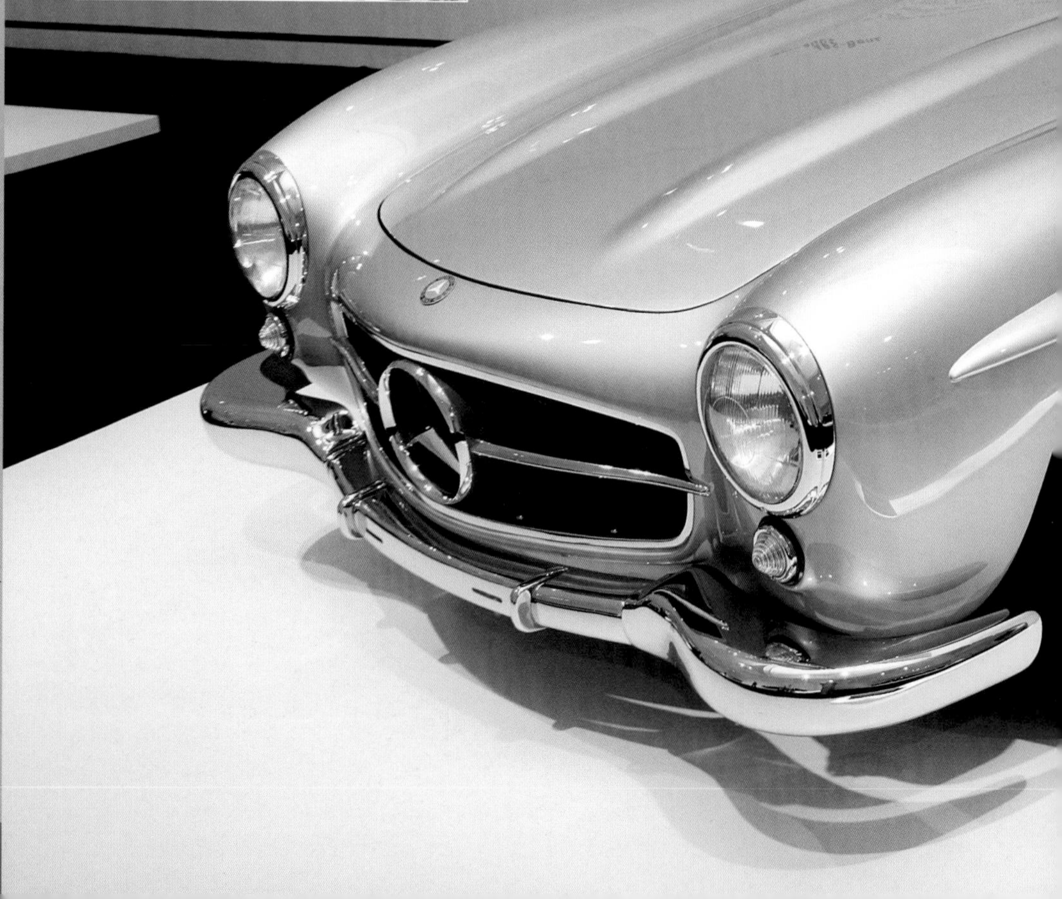

MERCEDES-BENZ 300SL

by Daimler and Benz
z AG and selling cars
. Although its factories
, this company was a
German economy and
uce cars that epitomize

NISSAN SKYLINE

This isn't so much about a car as a cult.

Although the United States is finally about to get its first Skyline GT-R for general sale, this famous Nissan supercar is already part of the automotive culture. To many fans, it's a car on a video game—like the *Gran Turismo* series—one that can beat the likes of Porsches and Ferraris on the screen, just as it can in real life.

To others, it's a quick glimpse they got of one, probably in an urban area. A used, right-hand-drive version that was imported from Japan and certified for the United States. Seeing a GT-R R34 snaking its way through traffic is as exciting, and as rare, as spotting a Lamborghini Murciélago.

That's Japan's famous Mt. Fuji in the background for this pair of Skylines. Thanks to its all-wheel-drive system, a Skyline is able to put its horsepower down on the ground, with the drive system also helping to make the handling balanced.

NISSAN SKYLINE

Price: est. $80,000 (1999 Skyline GT-R)
Engine: 280-horsepower, twin-turbo inline six
0–60 mph: 5.2 seconds
Top speed: 155 mph

Did You Know?

As with the new Skyline GT-R, the earlier Skylines have six-cylinder engines, though they are inline designs (the modern versions with turbochargers). Horsepower varied from model to model, and from tamer to racing versions, but it wasn't unusual to discover horsepower ratings from 280 to 600.

SHELBY GT350 & GT500

Racing legend Carroll Shelby worked out a deal with Ford to turn its Mustang pony car into a performance machine. Called the GT350, it had a 4.7-liter Ford V-8 that was modified to increase horsepower from 271 to 306. For a half decade, Shelby and Ford combined to build the GT350, the GT350H for the Hertz rental company, and the GT500 with its 7.0-liter V-8.

In their day, the Shelby GT350s were highly regarded for their performance, considering their sub-$4,500 price tags. It didn't hurt, of course, that they were able to play on the success of Shelby's mighty Cobras.

Shelby successfully raced the GT350 in its famous white-with-blue-stripes paint scheme. Now often used in vintage car racing, the purest of the racing GT350Rs will

SHELBY GT350 & GT500

Price: $4,428 (1966 Shelby GT350)
Engine: 306-horsepower, 4.7-liter V-8
0–60 mph: 7.3 seconds
Top speed: 124 mph

bring upwards of $1 million.

Performance tuners used Ford's new small V-8 extensively, though it never replaced the venerable small-block Chevrolet. While the first GT350s had the 4.7-liter V-8, as of 1968 it was replaced by a 5.0-liter, the famous Ford 302 V-8. Horsepower dropped to 250, though there was a 335-horsepower supercharged option.

Most of the GT350 interior was stock Mustang with important additions. An extra instrument pod on the dash included the tachometer. There was a wood-rim steering wheel and wide competition-style seat belts. It seems that most GT350s now have Carroll Shelby's autograph some place in the interior.

Did You Know?

Back in 1968, you could have bought a Shelby GT500 like the one on the next page for under $4,500, a bit more for the KR (King of the Road) version. Power would be 355 horsepower for the GT500, thanks to a 7.0-liter Ford V-8. These days, the same car in good condition would bring more than $150,000.

G.T.350
COBRA 428 JET
GT500
Radial T/A

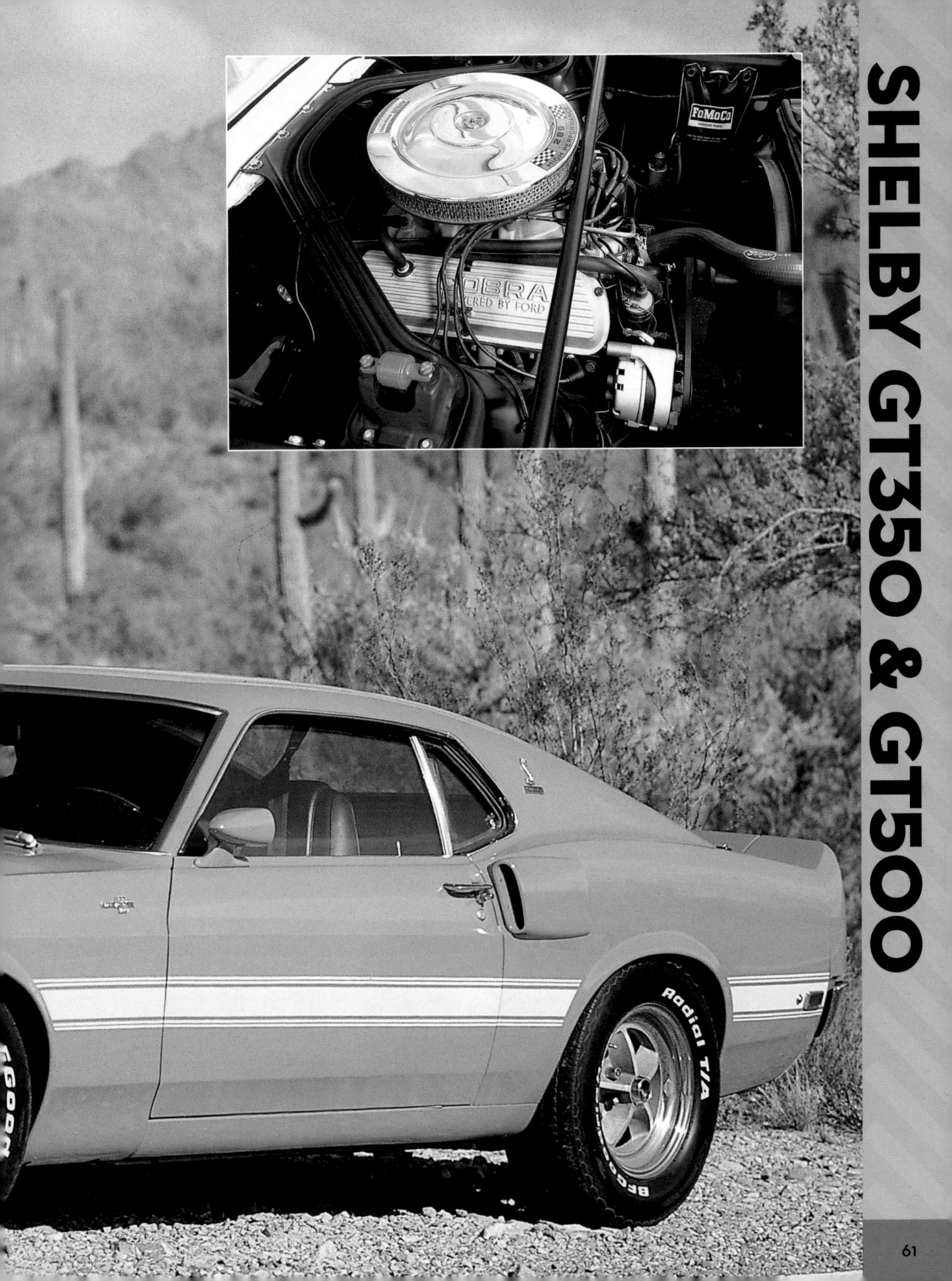
FoMoCo
289
HIGH PERFORMANCE
Radial T/A

CHAPTER 2

UP FRONT AUTOMO

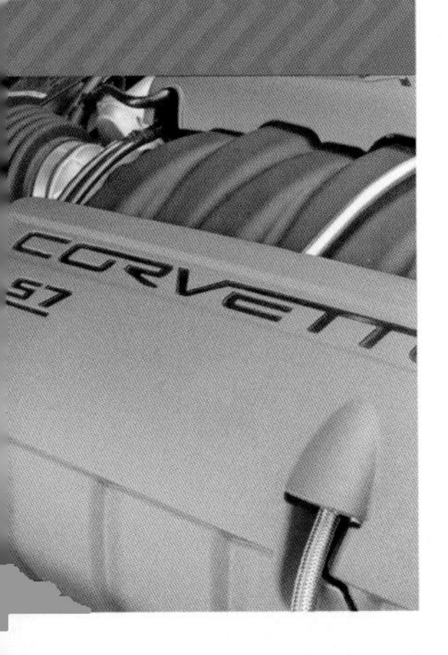

There are very sound reasons why our longest list of supercars is the one with front-mounted engines and rear- or all-wheel drive.

Arguably the best reason is money. It's very expensive to design and develop a new automobile, costs that these days can climb to more than $1 billion. So many of our favorite quick cars exist because they are a variation on a more commercial theme.

BMW's M Series cars are legends for their speed but wouldn't exist without the standard 3, 5, and 6 Series production cars.

We have the Cadillac XLR-V and Reeves Callaway's C16s thanks to Chevrolet building the Corvette, which itself has existed all these years because clever Chevy engineers knew how to raid the parts bin of more mundane machines to reconcile their sports car to the accountants.

Dodge Vipers owe their distinctiveness to a truck and its V-10, which was converted to work in the sports car. Henrik Fisker's coachbuilt machines wouldn't be around if it weren't for Mercedes-Benz's SLs and BMW's 6 Series.

Mercedes and AMG perform magic to create an entire lineup of supercars based on front-engine production products, and their one pure exotic, the McLaren-built SLR, is so front-engine it's a bit odd looking.

Production part considerations are also responsible for Saleen Mustangs, Nissan Skylines, and the fact that the latest Maseratis and the Alfa Romeo 8C are able to share components and thereby exist.

But there are also practicality and tradition to consider when doing a front-engine car with rear- or all-wheel drive. The packaging—engine-cockpit-trunk—makes sense. In the early 1970s, Ferrari was urged away from a front-engine layout for its big-engine supercar by the move to mid-engine race cars and by its great rival, Lamborghini. But after almost two decades of Berlinetta Boxers and Testarossas, the Italian firm went back to a front-engine design for its 550/575 and now 599 GTB because it makes more sense.

Aston Martins just wouldn't work as mid-engine machines . . . it would be like abandoning the monarchy in England, Aston's home country.

So while many fans of exotic cars are more tempted to "ohh and ahh" over mid-engine machines, give due respect to those with the powerplant up front. They are just as much fun.

Alfa Romeo is one of the most venerated automotive names in the world. The history of the Italian automaker is studded with famous race and street sports cars . . . but none in the United States since the mid-1990s. After more than a decade, Alfa returns to the States with its 8C Competizione.

What a beautiful way to come back. While the exterior design of the 8C certainly looks modern, anyone who knows Alfas of the past will see well-sculpted historic hints in the car's carbon-fiber bodywork.

ALFA ROMEO 8C

Price: est. $230,000
Engine: 450-horsepower, 4.7-liter V-8
0–60 mph: 4.2 seconds
Top speed: 181 mph

The wholesale use of carbon-fiber is one reason the 8C is pricey, probably bumping up on $250,000 when fully outfitted. Accompanying the coupe is an 8C Spider, which is just as beautiful . . . and quick.

Maserati and Ferrari supply the basics for the aluminum 32-valve V-8, which makes it to 450 horsepower and 354 lb-ft of torque in the Alfa. The six-speed paddle-shift manual gearbox is also shared with Maserati.

Like the V-8, the chassis of the 8C began with Maserati pieces . . . nothing wrong with that. The floorpan is a modified version of the Quattroporte's, with the suspension also adapted from the well-known sedan. In fact, 8Cs are assembled in the Maserati factory in Modena, Italy.

Anyone who has ever owned a modern Alfa recognizes the basic shape of the instrument pod in the 8C, which is packed with all the gauges. For the beautiful simplicity of the 8C's exterior, the interior is a bit busy looking, though it's nicely decked out in carbon-fiber (which is used for the seat shells), aluminum, and leather.

Did You Know?

The 8C in the Alfa's name stands for *otto cilindri*, Italian for eight cylinders.

auto
motor
-sport
auto
ILLUSTRIERTE

8C Competizione
8C Competizione

ASTON MARTIN DB7

After Ford bought a majority interest in Aston Martin in 1988, it began a program to update the British automaker's lineup with the DB7. Ian Callum penned the shape, creating something of a modern classic. The basis for the car came from Ford's stable, specifically Jaguar's stillborn F-Type.

First out was the 1993 DB7 coupe with its supercharged inline six, joined three years later by the convertible, which is always called the Volante model at Aston. With the V-12 engine in 1999, the coupe's name changed to Vantage, so the convertible became the Vantage Volante.

Aston Martin interiors have always been sumptuous, featuring soft leathers—often matched to contrasting piping—on comfortable seats with good side bolstering; thick carpeting; classic white-on-black gauges; and always plenty of rich wood trim.

Originally, the DB7s were powered by a Jaguar-based 3.2-liter supercharged inline six with 335 horsepower and 361 lb-ft of torque. Come 1999, it was replaced by a 5.9-liter V-12 with 420 horsepower and 400 lb-ft of torque. Both manual and automatic transmissions were offered.

ASTON MARTIN DB7

Price: $141,800 (coupe in 2003)
Engine: 420-horsepower, 5.9-liter V-12
0–60 mph: 5.0 seconds
Top speed: 184 mph

While the Aston's chassis may have started life as a potential Jaguar, no one cares when they hustle a DB7 into a curve. For despite the Aston's civilized ride—some argue a bit too civilized at high speed—handling on twisting roads is quite secure on the low-profile tires.

Did You Know?

Typical of Aston, there were variations on the theme, including 99 examples of the Zagato-bodied Vantage in 2003 and another 99 AR1s (American Roadster 1), also by Zagato and sold with no top.

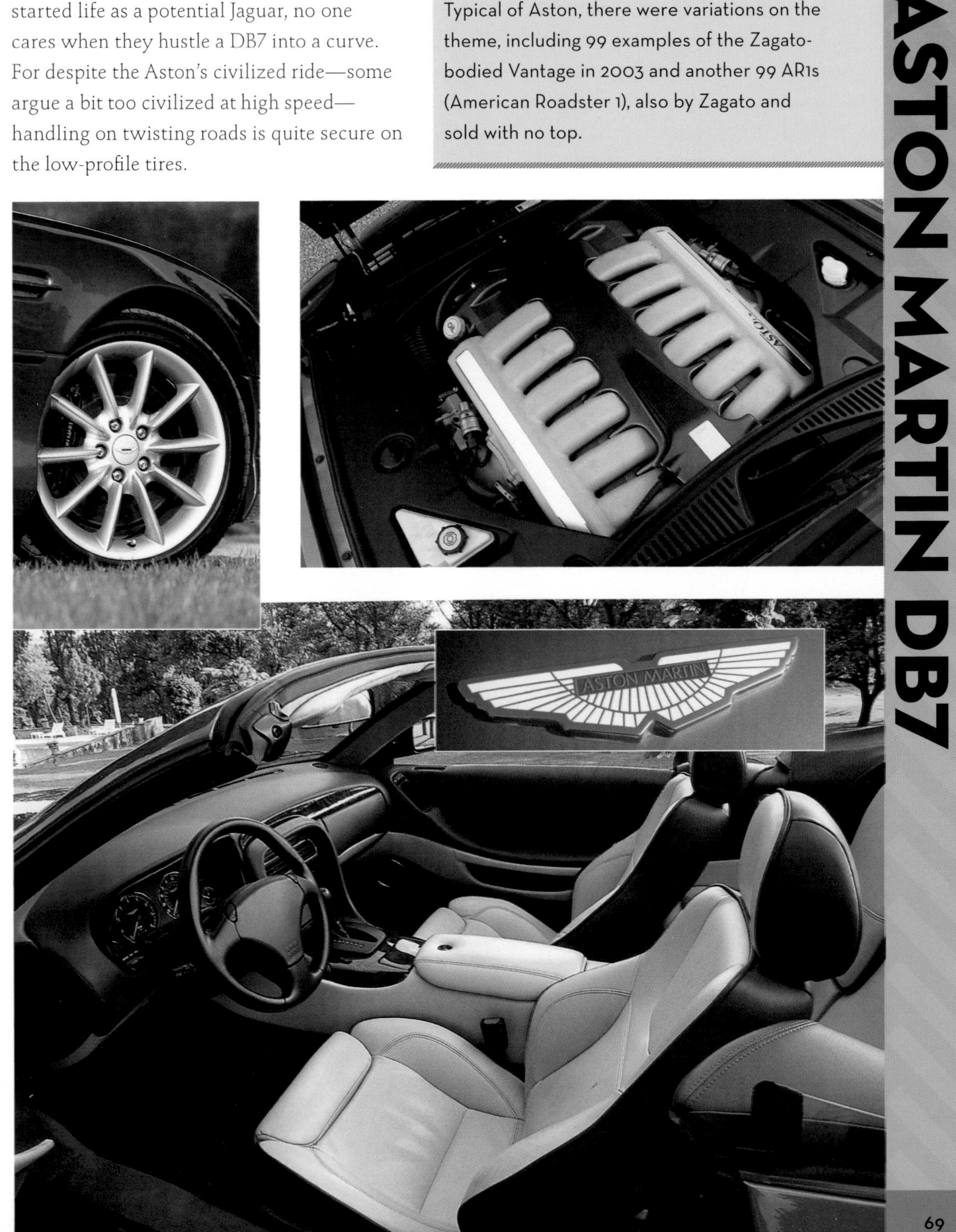

ASTON MARTIN DB9

Middle level in Aston Martin's three-strata model lineup is the DB9, successor to the DB7. Put in production in 2003, the DB9 is built as a coupe or convertible with bodywork first penned by noted Aston/ Jaguar designer Ian Callum and finished by Henrik Fisker (check out the Fisker cars in this book).

Like the DB7, the DB9 gets V-12 power, the aluminum powerplant pegged at 450 horsepower and 420 lb-ft of torque. Through a six-speed paddle transmission, the combo will go past 60 mph in 4.8 seconds, past 100 mph in 11.0 seconds, and through a quarter-mile in 13.2 seconds at 110 mph. Keep the hammer down, and you'll end up at 186 mph.

The interior of the Aston Martin DB9 LM pictured here is a special version that commemorates the DB9's 2007 Le Mans class win. Note how the controls are laid out logically from top to bottom, separating controls for audio and climate and including navigational and telephone systems.

DB9s are the basis for Aston Martin's racing efforts. Dubbed DBR9s, the cars', main competition comes from Corvette C6Rs and Saleen S7s. At the 2007 24 Hours of Le Mans, the Astons had their usual give-no-quarter battle with the Corvettes and came away class winners.

ASTON MARTIN DB9

Price: $169,750 (coupe), $183,250 (convertible)
Engine: 450-horsepower, 5.9-liter V-12
0–60 mph: 4.8 seconds
Top speed: est. 186 mph

Did You Know?

Both ends of the DB9 chassis have upper and lower A-arm suspensions, vented and slotted disc brakes, and Bridgestone tires on alloy wheels. Aston buyers can also have a "Sports Pack" that firms the car's structure and suspension and lowers ride height.

ASTON MARTIN V-8 VANTAGE

To compete against other exotic carmakers, Aston Martin felt it needed a three-tier model line. Star of the show, the high-priced DBS, and the DB9 take on Ferrari, while the $113,200 V-8 Vantage actually goes up against Porsche's 911 and Audi's R8.

Technically, the V-8 Vantage is something of a showcase starting with its bonded aluminum frame, which is encased in a body with aluminum, steel, and composite components. You can see elements of this structure under the hood and through the rear window, where they take on some of the elements of a motorcycle frame.

Some argue Aston is making a mistake linking all three of its models too closely visually, but you can't deny each is exciting.

Aston gave the V-8 Vantage an aluminum chassis and then added the expected upper and lower A-arm suspensions front and rear.

ASTON MARTIN V-8 VANTAGE

Price: $113,200
Engine: 380-horsepower, 4.3-liter V-8
0–60 mph: 4.7 seconds
Top speed: 175 mph

Big vented disc brakes lurk inside the 19-inch wheels that give the Aston such a great stance on the road. The transmission is rear mounted as a transaxle to give the car a near-even 49/51 weight distribution.

Aston has always done rather elegant interiors, though the V-8 Vantage is more toward the sporty, Porsche side—a somewhat simpler design but very efficient. If you prefer driving al fresco, you can also enjoy this interior in the $126,400 V-8 Vantage Roadster.

Did You Know?

Although Aston is one of the hallmark English specialists, the engine for the V-8 Vantage is assembled in Germany, as are the powerplants for the DB9 and DBS. Although it shares design elements with Jaguar's AJ-V-8, this is very much an Aston engine, sized at 4.3 liters and spinning to 380 horsepower and 303 lb-ft of torque.

ASTON MARTIN DBS

We saw it first in *Die Another Day* as James Bond's newest Aston Martin. At the 2007 Pebble Beach Concours we got to finally see the new DBS in the flesh . . . rather, in the carbon-fiber that makes up its fenders, hood, and rear deck. Looking like the spiffed up Vanquish it is, the DBS takes on a more muscular demeanor as the flagship of Aston's lineup. Under the carbon-fiber and aluminum bodywork is more structural aluminum in the 3,737-pound DBS.

The DBS has the technical creds to go with its buffed-up look: a powerful V-12 engine, six-speed manual or paddle-shifted semi-automatic gearbox, track-developed suspension, and the first carbon-ceramic brakes fitted to a road-going Aston.

Once thought of as elegant and fast but somewhat cumbersome, modern Astons

ASTON MARTIN DBS

Price: $265,000
Engine: 510-horsepower, 6.0-liter V-12
0–60 mph: 4.3 seconds
Top speed: 191 mph

have kept the first two qualities but jettisoned the latter.

While some critics say all Astons look too much alike, the changes made to transform the Vanquish to the DBS easily set it apart and up a rung from the DB9. And from the competition, which is Ferrari. Like the cars from Maranello, the exterior of the DBS has excellent detailing.

It may be a supercar, but the DBS has an interior that seems a bit more elegant than many exotics. That's part of the Aston tradition, bits like the aluminum controls on the black, polished surface of the center stack.

Did You Know?

Sourced in Cologne, Germany, the DBS V-12 is signed by its builder. It's an impressive-looking piece, fixed down below the Aston's cross-bay chassis stiffening bars, and the numbers go with the appearance: 510 horsepower and 420 lb-ft of torque . . . not to mention 0–60 mph in 4.3 seconds.

ASTON MARTIN DBS

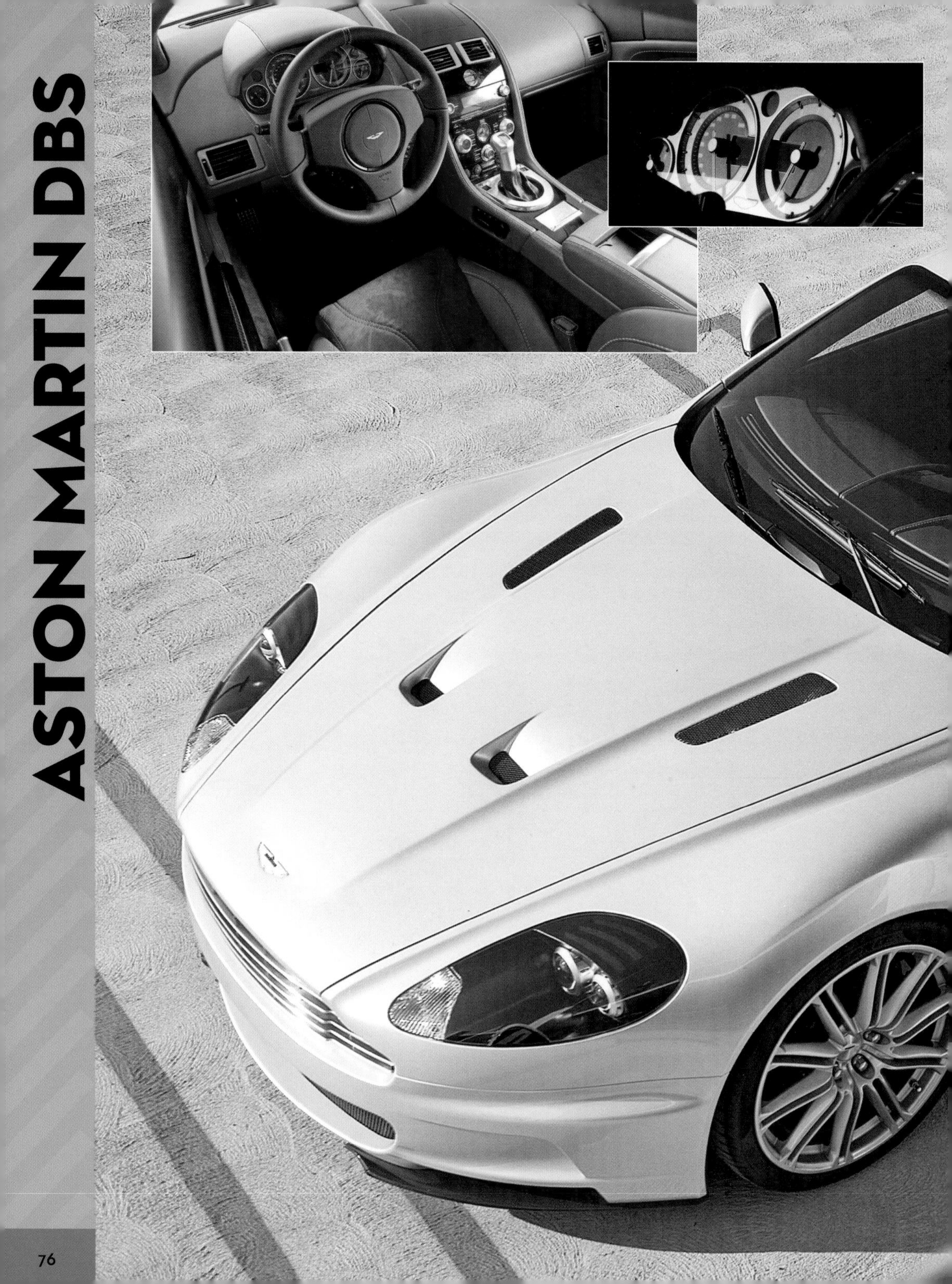

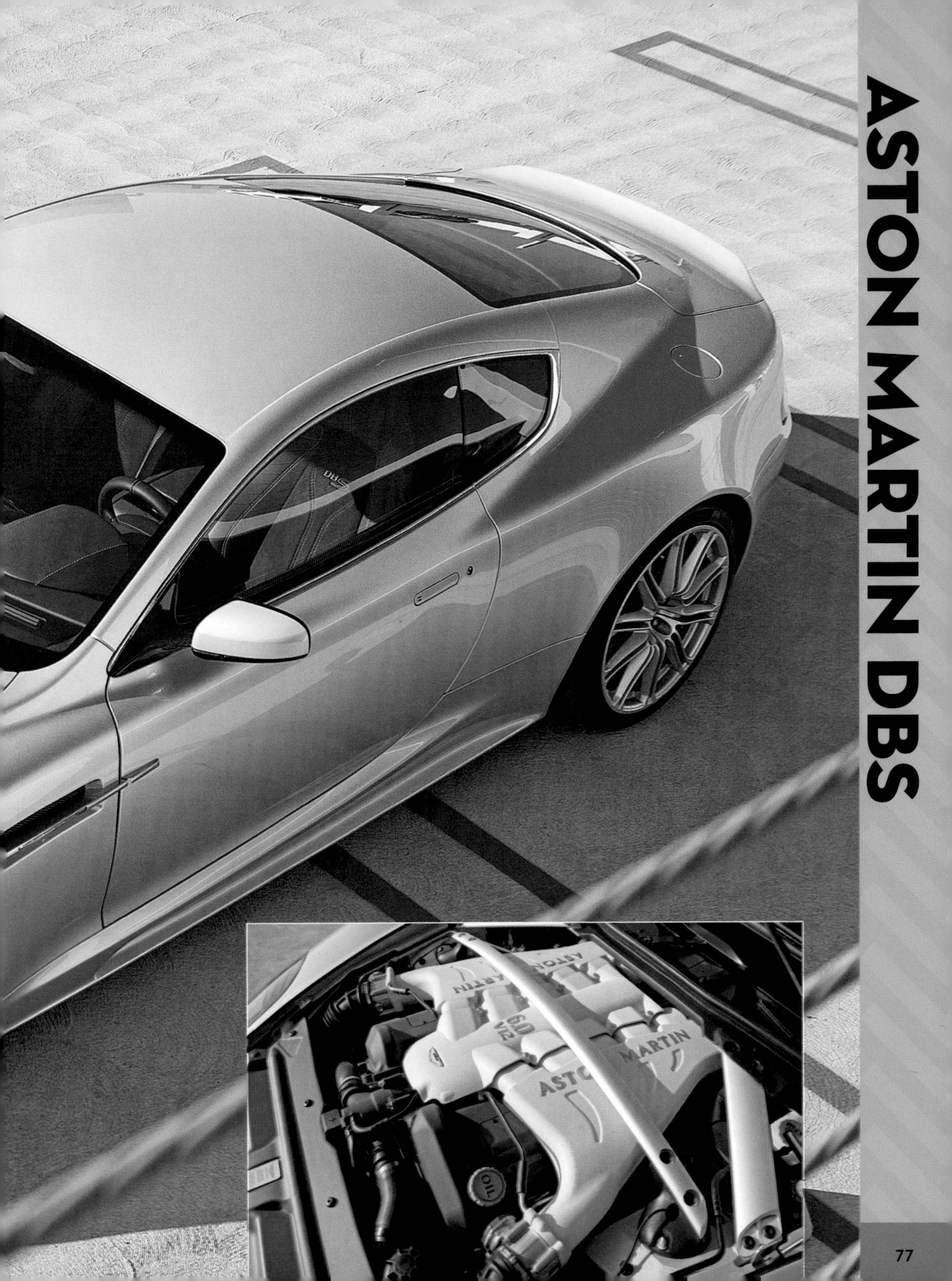
ASTON MARTIN
6.0 V12
OIL

It's one of the most enjoyable performance car segments in the business: the quick, small, Euro sedans from Audi (S4), Mercedes-Benz (C63), and the traditional sweetheart of the group, BMW's M3.

All are based on "normal" sedans that have been muscled with fender flares, larger wheels and tires, more aggressive noses, added vents, power dome hoods, spoilers, and engines that give new meaning to the need for traction control. And they look nastier, sitting down on lower, firmer suspensions.

BMW M3

Price: est. $60,000+
Engine: 414-horsepower, 4.0-liter V-8
0–60 mph: 4.6 seconds
Top speed: 155 mph (electronically limited), 175 mph (unlimited)

In the M3's case, all those changes mean these Bimmers get to 60 mph around 4.5 seconds, the quarter-mile coming up in about 12.5 seconds. And yet, despite their power-when-needed disposition, the M3s

can be quite civilized for daily driving, particularly the four-door sedan.

BMW first launched the M3 coupe, then the sedan, and later a convertible. All will have the same chassis with a MacPherson strut front suspension and independent multi-link rear design. The brakes are vented discs, and the M3s ride on 19-inch Michelin Pilot tires.

It isn't just the M logo in the tachometer that catches your eye, but also the (optimistic but encouraging) 200-mph speedometer. The engine redline is variable on the tach, starting low in a cool engine, then rotating to 8,400 rpm when the V-8 is warm.

Did You Know?
BMW says the aluminum 32-valve V-8 in M3s inherited technology from Formula 1, which makes sense when you determine it makes 1.5 horsepower per liter. That total of 414 is matched to 300 lb-ft of torque spread from 3,500 rpm to 7,000.

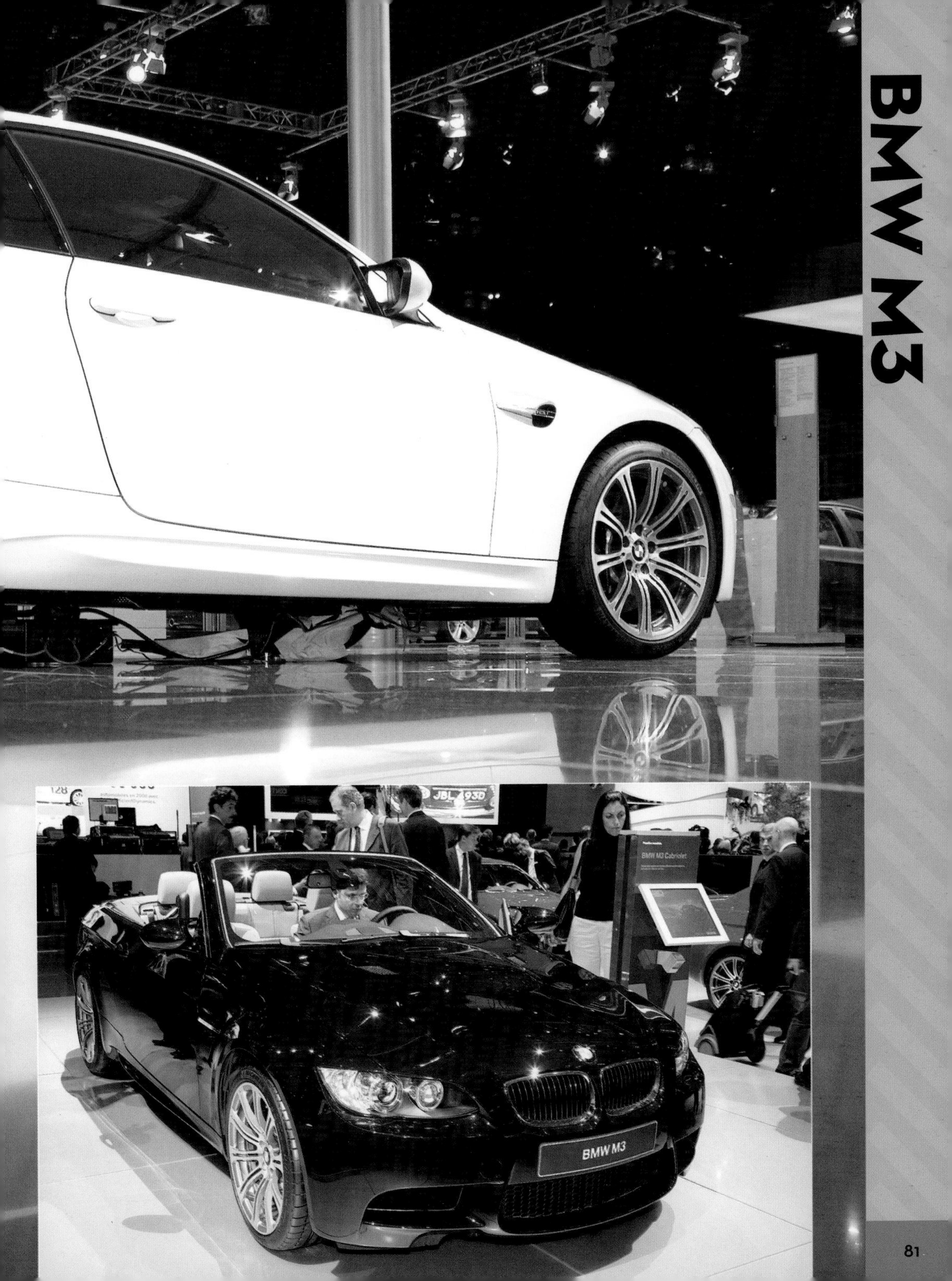
BMW M3 Cabriolet
BMW M3

BMW M5

Just say "M" around a BMW junkie, and you'll see eyes light up. These are, of course, the best Bimmer has to offer, and in the case of the M5, it starts—as in all M cars—under the hood. The 5.0-liter V-10 will rush the 4,100-pound four-door sedan to 60 mph in 4.1 seconds, to 100 in just 9.5.

Okay, the base price is $82,900, and you easily bump that into the mid-$90,000 range, but what great performance and a sort of square-shoulder elegance.

It would be difficult to criticize the ride and handling dynamics of the M5. The MacPherson strut front and multi-link suspensions keep the V-10's super performance under control. And to stop the BMW from its 155-mph computer-trimmed top speed are large, vented, cross-drilled disc brakes.

BMW M5

Price: $82,900

Engine: 500-horsepower, 5.0-liter V-10

0–60 mph: 4.1 seconds

Top speed: 155 mph (electronically limited)

Where the fun happens: the driver's seat of the M5. Materials are top quality and beautifully finished. Great detailing includes bits like lighted "+" and "–" signs on the shift paddles. Only downside to the layout is the dreaded iDrive.

Here's what all the fuss is about: BMW's 5.0-liter V-10. The German automaker slots horsepower in at 500 and torque at 383 lb-ft. The seven-speed paddle-shifted automatic is excellent at speed but a bit clunky for around-town driving.

Did You Know?

There aren't many clues to visually separate an M5 from its 550i corporate brother (other than $35,000 more on the price tag), but there is also an air and presence about the M5 that is strength personified.

BMW M6

If you like BMW's M5, but prefer a coupe instead of the 5's four-door sedan body, BMW would be happy to sell you an M6. Externally they are quite different, sharing only BMW's signature kidney grilles and their Chris Bangle–inspired designs. Inside are the same components: tight gauge package, excellent M Sport Seats, and, like it or not, iDrive.

Underneath all that, the BMW pair has the same drivetrain with its 500-horsepower V-8 and seven-speed sequential transmission, right down to identical gear ratios. At just shy of 3,800 pounds, the coupe is some 250 pounds lighter than the sedan, but the pair shares the same acceleration numbers up to 70 mph, where the coupe creeps ahead so that by 120 mph it's leading by a half-second.

BMW M6

Price: $99,100 (coupe), $104,900 (convertible)
Engine: 500-horsepower, 5.0-liter V-10
0–60 mph: 4.1 seconds
Top speed: 155 mph (electronically limited)

M5 or M6 you get the same solid, secure handling, thanks to aluminum-component independent suspensions front and rear with M Driving Dynamics Control. And both get the same huge, vented, cross-drilled disc brakes. Ride in the pair is not freeway smooth but quite acceptable, given their handling potential.

The interior is a nice place to be while enjoying your M6. The leather is top notch, the fit and finish tight and well done. Major carbon-fiber trim is an option, as is the excellent heads-up display system.

The highly regarded V-10 from BMW, with its 5.0 liters, 500 horsepower, and 383 lb-ft of torque, is the heart of it. Shifting is by way of a manual seven-speed that is sequentially shifted by steering wheel paddles, though you can set the transmission to shift automatically. Quick shifting at speed but cumbersome in day-to-day driving.

Did You Know?
An interesting detail: The tachometer's redline rises as the engine warms up.

BMW
The Ultimate Driving Machine

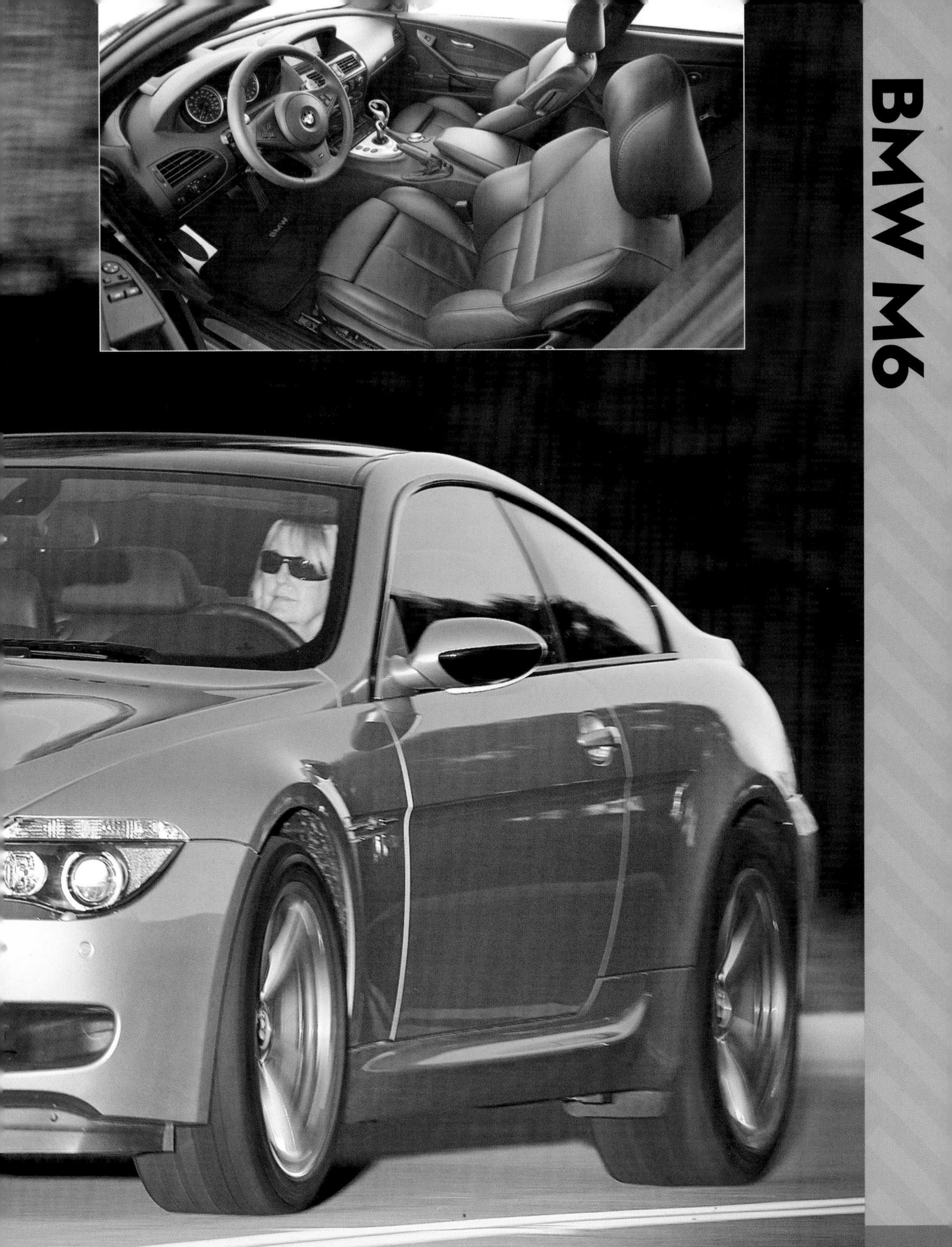

BMW M6

When Cadillac decided it needed a sports machine to compete against rivals Mercedes-Benz and Jaguar, it turned inside General Motors for help.

With Chevrolet producing the best Corvettes ever, Caddy used that sports car as the basis for what it calls the XLR. It shares the 'Vette's rigid, lightweight frame right down to the center aluminum tunnel, composite floorboards, and 105.7-inch wheelbase. Ditto with the aluminum A-arm suspensions and transverse composite leaf springs.

CADILLAC XLR

Price: $97,860
Engine: 443-horsepower, 4.4-liter, supercharged V-8
0–60 mph: 4.3 seconds
Top speed: 155 mph (electronically limited)

Naturally, Cadillac uses its own Northstar V-8 to power the XLR, which is covered in a squarish-style body that is in contrast to the shape of the Corvette.

When it felt it needed a more potent sports car, Caddy supercharged the V-8 and created

the XLR-V, a competitor for the Mercedes AMG SL55 and Jaguar's XJR.

With the added horsepower of the supercharged V-8, Cadillac firmed up the independent suspension of the XLR-V. The Magnetic Ride Control shocks have been firmed and a rear anti-roll bar added. Brakes are the same big discs fitted to the Corvette Z51. Driven hard, the XLR-V is well mannered and quite capable against its European competition.

Cadillac mounted a quiet-running Roots-type supercharger with an integrated intercooler atop the Northstar V-8. This is an elegant design package that boosts horsepower to 443 at 6,499 rpm and torque to 414 lb-ft, most of it between 2,200 and 6,000 rpm. The transmission is a rear-mounted six-speed automatic.

Did You Know?

As expected in a Cadillac, the XLR-V's interior is a mix of sport and luxury. Bulgari designed the instruments, the trim is Zingana wood, and the seats are finished in fine, stitched leather. In foul weather, a folded hardtop can be erected at a button's push to turn the roadster into a well-sealed coupe.

CADILLAC XLR

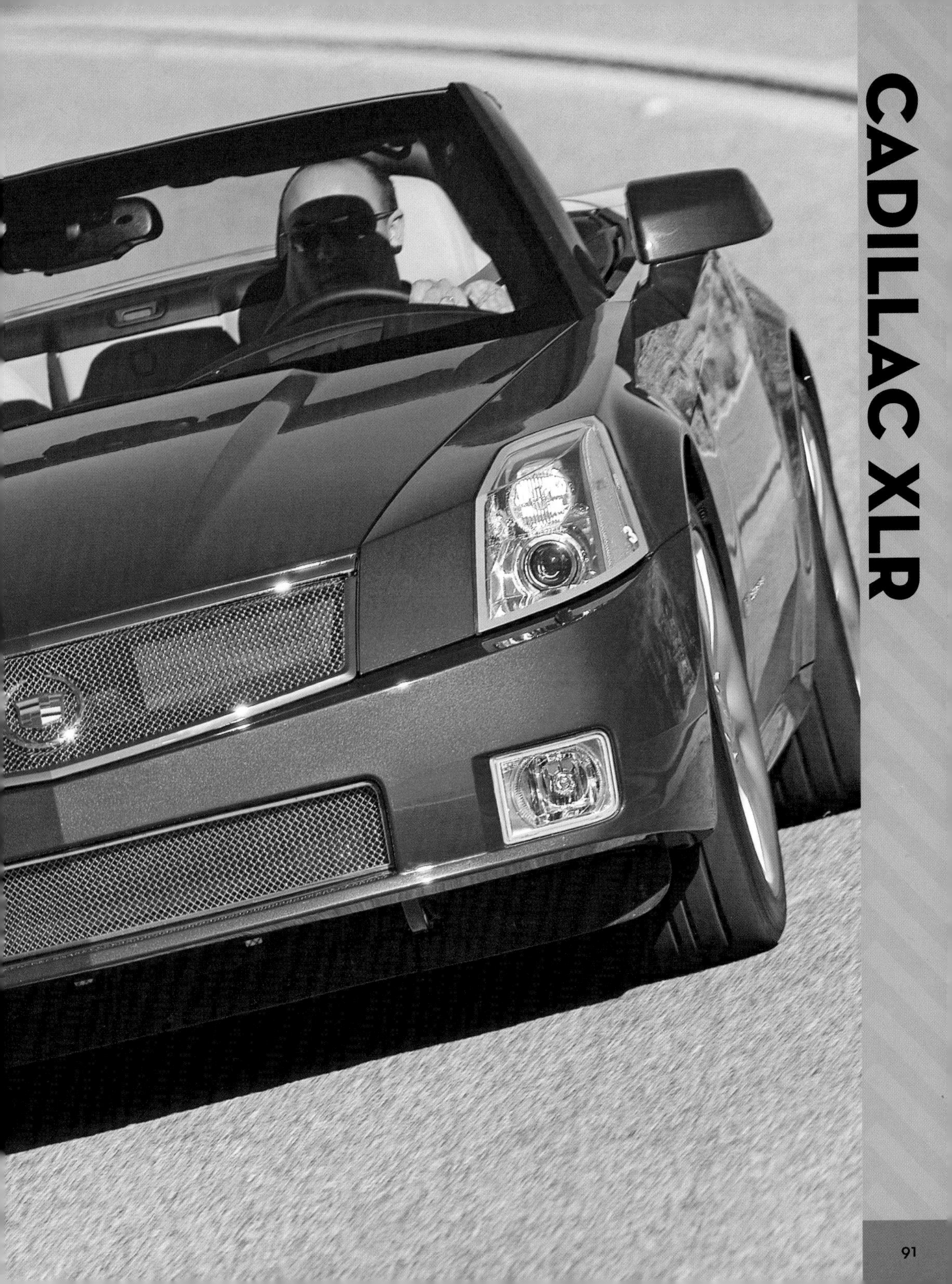

For decades, Reeves Callaway has been turning otherwise very nice Corvettes into still-quicker machines. There have been 16 generations of such supercars, hence the name C16 for his latest.

The most striking feature is new bodywork, which is traditionally drawn for Callaway by Canadian Paul Deutschman. The Corvette grille is replaced with one that hints at the classic Ferrari egg-crate style, but with a smile. All the removable body panels are new as you work to the back, past the brake vents, and to the rear single-taillight-per-side back end. While the standard roof is retained, there are new rear quarter panels with a bit of the buttresses found in Ferrari's 599 GTB.

But what really makes a Callaway a Callaway is under that pronounced hood

CALLAWAY C16

Price: $192,180
Engine: 616-horsepower, 6.0-liter, supercharged V-8
0–60 mph: 3.3 seconds
Top speed: est. 206 mph

bulge: a supercharged V-8. And a price tag that can run to near $200,000.

Callaway appreciates the engineering that goes into the Corvette, so the base C16 has the Z51 suspension option from the 'Vette's option list. Callaway also offers its own variation. Called the Callaway/Eibach Multi-Pro coil-over suspension, it has, among other features, unique adjustable shock absorbers and Callaway's own front and rear anti-sway bars.

At 560 horsepower and 529 lb-ft of torque, the base Callaway supercharged 6.0-liter V-8 is powerful enough for most drivers. But there is an upgrade to a tire-twisting 616 horsepower and 582 lb-ft of torque. In either case, you can twin the V-8 with a manual or automatic six-speed gearbox.

Did You Know?

In its quest for horsepower, Callaway doesn't ignore creature comforts. The interior goes upmarket . . . fixing one of the few complaints about the C6 Corvette. But wait, there's more, like the optional Deutschleder interior featuring German leather ($24,300) and/or the lightweight Sportseat package with its shell seats at $6,940 for the pair.

CALLAWAY C16

CALLAWAY

CALLAWAY C16 SPEEDSTER

If Reeves Callaway's C16 at around $192,000 is a bit too mundane for you, order one of his C16 Speedsters. As you can see, it's totally devoid of a top . . . any top. You can't get one. Instead you nestle behind a pair of small windscreens, Callaway advising a helmet at anything above 35 mph.

Callaway has done Speedsters before, and they are a rare breed . . . and expensive, with a price tag just about $300,000. Pricey, but with a great bag of tricks, from the 616-horsepower supercharged V-8 to the lightweight carbon-fiber road wheels.

Speed rises in the Speedster, and the occupants' hearing begins to buzz as air rushes by. Do this long enough, and you'll begin to suffer a receding hairline. So Callaway built a pair of lightweight, carbon-fiber helmets into the design under a pop-up rear panel.

CALLAWAY C16 SPEEDSTER

Price: $305,000
Engine: 616-horsepower, 6.0-liter, supercharged V-8
0–60 mph: 3.8 seconds
Top speed: est. 206 mph

The big rear taillights and flared headrests . . . for most drivers this is the view you would get of the C16 as it rushes away from you. Notice there are no exterior door handles? Just run your hand over the top rear of each door and it pops open.

Ah, the heart of any Callaway, the supercharged V-8. The C16 Speedster has the 616-horsepower version with its specific cylinder heads and bigger valves. The supercharger is mounted "backwards," being spun from the rear of the engine to give incoming air a straight shot into the blower.

Did You Know?

Unlike the old days when many supercars were quick but fragile, this, like all Callaways, is covered by a mix of General Motors and Callaway warranties for five years/100,000 miles on the advanced powertrain.

CHRYSLER FIREPOWER CONCEPT

It seemed like a no-brainer, a natural, a "no kidding, Sherlock" decision. If Dodge had been successful with the V-10-powered Viper, why not do a Chrysler version? It could use the same chassis but would have to be different . . . more sophisticated . . . but it could work.

So Chrysler presented the Firepower at the 2005 Detroit Auto Show to great applause. You could tell by the very-long-hood, short-deck proportions that it was Viper underneath, but that was it. Up front was a typical Chrysler grille, and you could see hints of the mid-engine ME Four-Twelve in the details. In total, a quite elegant design.

But stalled in the gates, as it turned out. Great shape, good press, plenty of enthusiasm, but a shaky business case.

How sad.

In contrast to the Viper's sporty interior, the Firepower's is more elegant and a bit nautical. The colors are oyster white and ocean blue with black lacquer and chrome detailing. There's a bright and open feeling thanks to a glass roof. Like all Chrysler concept cars, the Firepower was finished to full production quality.

Chrysler figured the V-10 was Viper property and not really the sort of engine you'd like in a sophisticated Grand Touring car. So engineers opted for the SRT-8 version of Chrysler's 6.1-liter Hemi V-8 that provides 425 horsepower and 420 lb-ft of torque. The transmission is a Chrysler five-speed automatic with AutoStick shifting.

CHRYSLER FIREPOWER CONCEPT

Price: Not Applicable
Engine: 425-horsepower, 6.1-liter V-8
0–60 mph: est. 4.5 seconds
Top speed: est. 175 mph

Did You Know?

Overall the Firepower is 3 inches shorter and about an inch taller than the Viper. Chrysler estimated production weight at around 3,380 pounds thanks in part to a carbon-fiber body. At that, the automaker figured the Hemi's torque would get that package to 60 mph in just 4.5 seconds.

CORVETTE 2009 ZR1

In the end, even the ZO6 wasn't enough for the speed merchants at Chevrolet. They wanted a Corvette that could outrun all the major supercars in the world. We heard rumors of this new machine for some time, its nickname being "Blue Devil," thanks to the color of its prototypes being tested in Germany on the Nürburgring.

Externally, the major differences include the carbon-fiber hood with its window over the V-8. Carbon-fiber is also used for front fenders with new vents, the roof panel, front splitter, and rocker panels. At the back is a larger full-width spoiler.

Even with the hood down, you'll be allowed to view the supercharged V-8 through a polycarbonate window. Chevy passed on a larger displacement V-8, instead adding an Eaton supercharger to whomp the 6.2-liter, LS9 V-8 to 620 horsepower and 595 lb-ft of torque. Gearbox is a six-speed manual.

CORVETTE 2009 ZR1

Price: $100,000
Engine: 620-horsepower supercharged 6.2-liter V-8
0–60 mph: est. 3.2 seconds
Top speed: 200+ mph

With the added power comes increased chassis management, beginning with Magnetic Selective Ride Control. The tires are Michelin Pilot Sport 2s, sized P285/30ZR-19 front and P335/25ZR-20 rear. Inside those alloy wheels are the same carbon-ceramic brakes use on Ferrari's Enzo (the fronts) and FXX (the rears).

Little changes inside the ZR1 from the ZO6, including the lightweight seats but with ZR1 badging. There are two important additions, a 220-mph speedometer and a boost gauge. Blower pressure can also be seen in the heads-up instrument display in the windshield.

Did You Know?

It may cost $100,000, but the new ZR1 boosts a better power-to-weight ratio than Porsche's GT2, Ferrari's 599, and Lamborghini's big LP640 . . . and you can't get them for $100,000.

CORVETTE Z06

It seems odd to write about value-per-dollar and 0–60 mph in 3.9 seconds, but that's what you get with the Corvette Z06. Its performance figures—the 0–60 time, 0–100 in 8.8 seconds, the quarter-mile in 12.2 seconds at 120.7 mph, and that 198-mph top speed—are the stuff of exotics that cost tens of thousands of dollars more. Then you can snick the Corvette into sixth gear and cruise along at 70-plus mph getting around 30 mpg.

The Z06 interior was obviously penned by designers who enjoy driving, because it is configured for hard driving, though it also makes a comfortable cruiser.

What else would be at the heart of a Corvette other than a honkin' pushrod, two-valve-per-cylinder V-8? And the finely developed powerplant—with what some automakers call old tech—delivers 505 horsepower and 470 lb-ft of torque through a six-speed manual transmission.

CORVETTE Z06

Price: $70,175
Engine: 505-horsepower, 7.0-liter V-8
0–60 mph: 3.9 seconds
Top speed: 198 mph

Ancient Corvettes were chided for having somewhat crude handling, but that complaint is long gone, modern 'Vettes as capable as their European competition. The Chevy sports car's one technical oddity: transverse leaf springs. Through the alloy wheels you can see the drilled and vented disc brakes.

Okay, it's not a Z06, but this carbon fiber black 'Vette (bottom, opposite) comes from Pratt & Miller, which builds the race-winning factory C6R Corvettes. One of a batch of 25, the C6RS has an 8.2-liter, 600-horsepower V-8 . . . and, yes, that is its owner, Jay Leno, with the black beast.

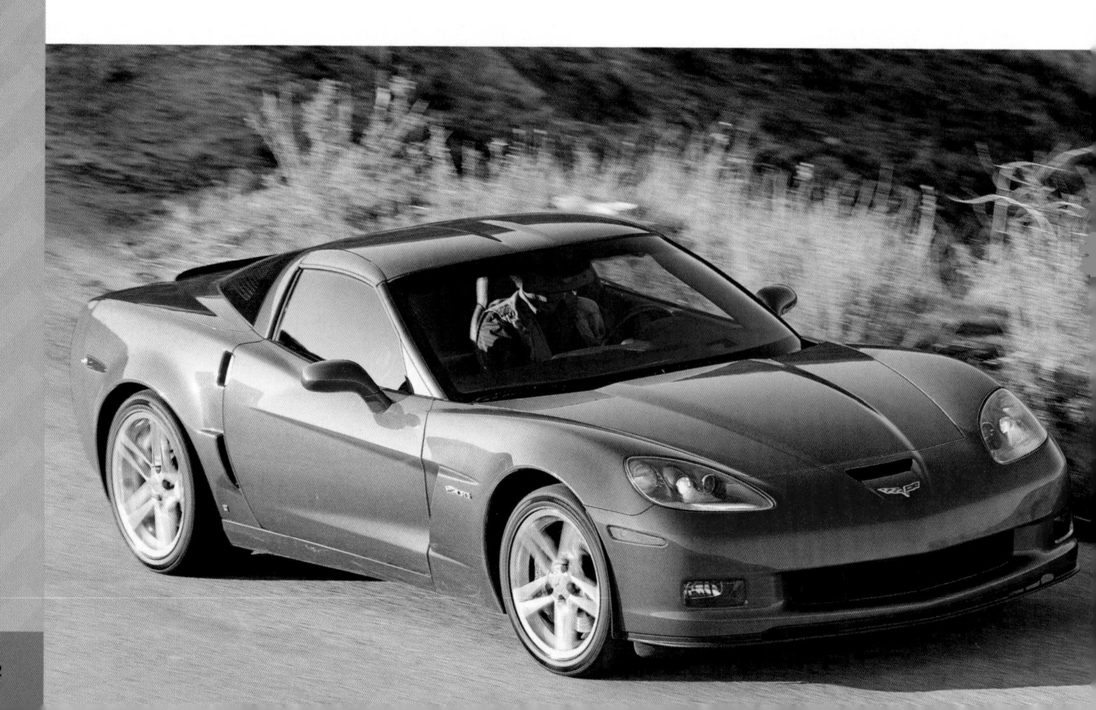

Did You Know?

As comedian and ZO6 owner Jay Leno points out, because it's a Chevrolet, the sports car is not only reliable but, heaven forbid something happens, the Corvette is easy and inexpensive to fix.

It was a powerful combination of men like Bob Lutz, Carroll Shelby, and designer Tom Gale that got the Viper into the real world. Chrysler was looking to boost its image, so it recreated its V-10 truck engine in aluminum, developed a proper chassis, and clothed the sports car in a plastic composite body that would steal your heart.

We saw the first design study at the 1989 Detroit Auto Show, and reaction was so positive that by January 1992, the car had been developed and was on sale.

DODGE VIPER 1991-2002

Price: $50,000 (1992)
Engine: 400-horsepower, 8.0-liter V-10
0–60 mph: 4.8 seconds
Top speed: 160 mph

Early Vipers are crude beasts in some ways, with side curtains and a rudimentary top, but good gravy do they deliver the goods, bellowing their way to 60 mph in less than 5 seconds. You're never bored in a Viper.

If the original Viper was a bit basic for some drivers, the GTS coupe is a tamer device . . . it even has glass side windows. The GTS had a successful career on the racetrack. Vipers won their class in the 24 Hours of Le Mans from 1998 to 2000 and that latter year took an overall win in the Rolex 24 at Daytona.

The very early Viper debuted back in the days before driver and passenger air bags. There was never anything complicated about the sports car's interior: Simple black-on-white gauges spread out for easy reading. The plain-looking seats are quite comfortable.

Did You Know?

Lamborghini, which was owned by Chrysler at the time, did some of the early work in converting the truck V-10 to aluminum. The first iteration of the big 8.0-liter engine delivered 400 horsepower and 450 lb-ft of torque, though in 1996, horsepower went to 450.

DODGE VIPER 1991–2002

VIPER
DODGE
MICHELIN

Come 2003, the Dodge Viper SRT10 was ready for a redesign. The exterior fundamentals remained but with a sharper, edgier look. Initially, only the convertible was done, but two years later, the coupe (formerly the GTS) was launched, retaining much of the look of the older version from the door rearward.

Engineers managed to trim weight from the aluminum and steel chassis and yet make it stiffer. Suspensions are still upper and lower A-arm designs front and rear, and there are 14.0-inch-diameter disc brakes all around.

The thrumming rumble of the Viper's V-10 is a rather unique sound in the exotic car world. When the 2003 Viper was introduced, the big pushrod engine was at 8.3 liters with 510 horsepower and 535 lb-ft of torque. For 2008, the displacement went out to 8.4 liters, horsepower to an even 600, and torque jumping to 560 lb-ft.

DODGE VIPER 2003-PRESENT

Price: $84,745
Engine: 600-horsepower, 8.4-liter V-10
0–60 mph: 3.7 seconds
Top speed: 202 mph

Viper interiors have always been kept simple, the fundamental gauges laid out for the driver to easily read. You sit nestled into the seats, held in place laterally by the high center console that covers the Tremec TR6060 six-speed manual gearbox.

Convertible or coupe, the Viper is a stormer, with 60 mph a short 3.7 seconds away from launch. Then comes 100 mph in 8.4 seconds. There's nothing subtle about this, the trip to 100 coming with all the thunder and drama you'd expect from a 600-horsepower car called Viper.

Did You Know?

Racing continues to be an important part of the Viper program, and at the 2007 Los Angeles Auto Show, Dodge debuted the ACR version with numerous aerodynamic additions, including a tall rear wing.

DODGE VIPER ACR

Dodge Vipers have a glorious racing history, not only taking an overall victory in the Rolex 24 at Daytona, but also class honors at Le Mans and countless wins in smaller races.

Dodge wants to keep the momentum going, so it provides a version called ACR, for American Club Racer. Not only does it look very cool, but the ACR version comes race ready and 40 pounds lighter than the stock Viper. There's also a Hard Core option that cuts another 40 pounds by deleting such amenities as the radio, carpeting, and much of the sound deadening.

DODGE VIPER ACR

Price: est. $95,000
Engine: 600-horsepower, 8.4-liter V-10
0–60 mph: est. 3.5 seconds
Top speed: 202 mph

While it is street legal, you'd be hard pressed to drive the ACR on the street and retain your hearing . . . but wouldn't it be fun?

To make certain the ACR meets production car rules, the engine is left stock. That's probably enough, given that the 8.4-liter V-10 has 600 horsepower and 560 lb-ft of torque. Behind the V-10 is a rugged Tremec T56 six-speed gearbox.

Among the aerodynamic changes for the Viper ACR is the tall carbon-fiber spoiler. Up front is a carbon-fiber splitter to route the air, plus an added extender for track use only that further increases from downforce.

Did You Know?
To make the ACR adjustable for the racetrack, it is fitted with a German coil-over suspension along with a larger front anti-sway bar. Michelin supplies the Pilot Sport Cup tires, and the car has special two-piece rotors for its large disc brakes.

BAU 0805
DODGE
VIPER
POSITIVE

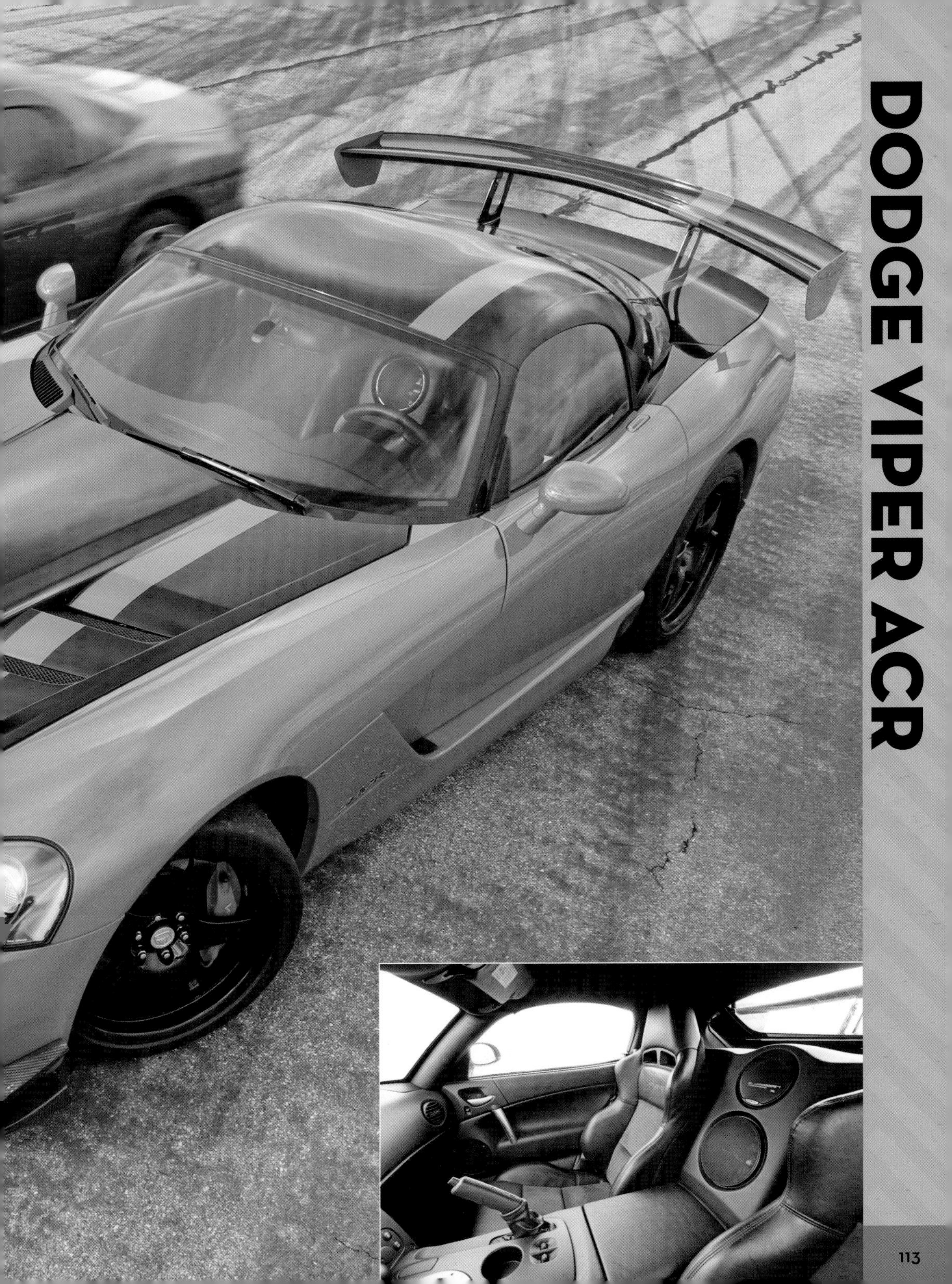

FERRARI 550/575M/BARCHETTA

Many Ferrari fans were relieved when the Italian automaker replaced its Testarossa with the 1996 550 Maranello. The mid-engine "TR" sporting a huge backside was a bit ungainly. With the front-engine 550, Ferrari returned to the sort of V-12 supercar category it left when the Daytona went out of production.

FERRARI 550/575M/ BARCHETTA

Price: $212,000
Engine: 515-horsepower, 5.7-liter V-12
0–60 mph: 4.7 seconds
Top speed: 200 mph

After using a flat 12 for its Boxer and Testarossa exotic cars, Ferrari returned to a V-12 for the 550 Maranello. The twin-cam, 48-valve, 5.5-liter engine got the nod at 485 horsepower and 419 lb-ft of torque. Revised for the 575M Maranello for 2002, the engine went to 5.75 liters, 515 horsepower, and 434 lb-ft of torque. That 4.7-seconds-to-60 time was quite good in 1996, as was the top speed of 200 mph, but what also impressed was the

combination of racetrack-quality handling with a very acceptable down-the-road ride.

At the 2000 Paris Auto Show, Ferrari pulled the lid off a convertible version of the 550 Maranello called the Barchetta. The latter means "little boat" and was the nickname of a famous early Ferrari body style. A true roadster, the top that comes with the car is for speeds below 70 mph. A total of 448 Barchettas were produced.

For all their sportiness, Ferraris never lack for style and quality in their interiors. The 550/575 were in the pre-carbon-fiber-trim days and have acres of leather on the seats and dashboard. These were the first of the truly modern street Ferraris with efficient sound and heating/air conditioning systems that work efficiently.

Did You Know?

Presented to the press at Germany's Nürburgring, where the likes of Michael Schumacher and Max Papis gave blistering rides, the 550 quickly proved it was more than the equivalent of the mid-engine Testarossa.

0 20 40 60 80 100 120 140 160 180 200 220 240 260 280 300 320 340
km/h
1 2 3 4 5 6 7 8 9 10
130

For more than 35 years, Ferrari has had a high-performance 2+2 machine, its latest being the 612 Scaglietti. That second name is to honor Sergio Scaglietti, the legendary bodymaker who clothed many famous Ferraris.

There's no denying the 612's styling is controversial. Ferrari and its long-time design house, Pininfarina, often dip into history for styling elements. Here they adapted—not too successfully—the side sculpting off a famous special-bodied 375 MM bought by director Roberto Rossellini for actress Ingrid Bergman.

As an example of how reliable Ferraris are these days, several of us were involved in a project in which we drove 612 Scagliettis through China. On the next page, the pair is seen on the highest paved road in the world,

FERRARI 612 SCAGLIETTI

Price: $269,829
Engine: 532-horsepower, 5.7-liter V-12
0–60 mph: 4.6 seconds
Top speed: 199 mph

at over 17,000 feet, where they operated flawlessly.

Not only does Ferrari's V-12 look terrific with its red crackle paint finish, but it has the power to go with the appearance. The 5.7-liter V-12 sports 48 valves, is beautifully honed from aluminum, and sends you 532 horsepower and 434 lb-ft of torque. That's enough to hurl this 4,300-pound car to 60 mph in 4.6 seconds.

Now many automakers have manual transmissions with no clutch pedal or shift lever but send you from gear to gear by way of paddles ahead of the steering wheel. Ferrari was the leader, and its F1 system is still the best. When it offered the transmission on the 612 Scaglietti, it was the first time Ferrari matched it to a V-12.

Did You Know?

Ferrari made this a proper 2+2 so an adult, in a squeeze, can fit in back. The result is a rather long car, stretching 193 inches nose to tail. Even squeezed inside, it's a great place to be, all cocooned in leather.

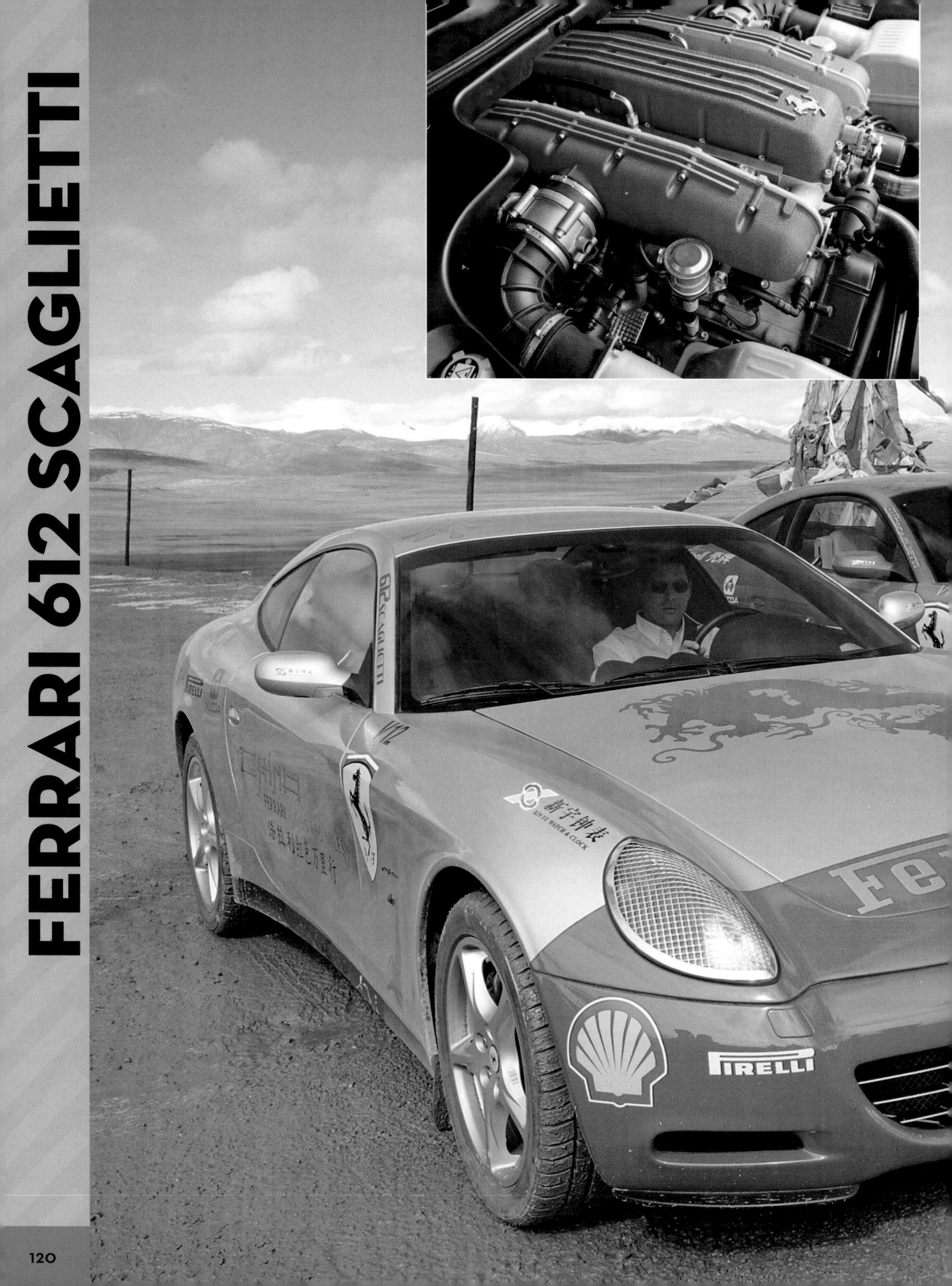
612 SCAGLIETTI
V12
PIRELLI

OFF
AUTO
UP
Ferrari
法拉利
PIRELLI
www.ferrariworld.com

FERRARI 599 GTB FIORANO

After its mid-engine interlude when the Berlinetta Boxer and Testarossa reigned, Ferrari went back to a front-engine "big car" with the 550/575 Maranello. That was a very nice machine, but its successor, the 2007 599 GTB Fiorano, is a barnburner.

It begins with the Ferrari's heart-tugging Pininfarina bodywork, which features a classic egg-crate grille, purposeful vents, and little flying buttresses at the back of the greenhouse. Inside are leather-covered seats that are comfy enough for your living room but equally suited to hard driving.

The latter would include not just getting to 60 mph in 3.2 seconds and a top speed of

FERRARI 599 GTB FIORANO

Price: $264,034

Engine: 620-horsepower, 6.0-liter V-12

0–60 mph: 3.2 seconds

Top speed: 205 mph

205 mph, but near-perfect handling on any sort of road you cover along the way.

Ah, nothing says Ferrari like a V-12. In the 599, it's in aluminum with a pair of camshafts on each cylinder head. At a displacement of 6.0 liters, Ferrari says the V-12 has 620 horsepower at 7,600 rpm and 448 lb-ft of torque at 5,600.

The comfy side of the Ferrari 599 is the leather-upholstered interior. Note the carbon-fiber trim and the hooded instrument cluster with its red speedometer (you can also choose yellow). On the steering wheel are the red "START" button and the *manettino* that adjusts the car's performance.

Did You Know?

Almost all exotic carmakers have paddle-shifted transmissions, but at Ferrari it has become an art form. Called the F1 gearbox, it pops paddle shifts faster than you can blink, one reason the 599 gets to 60 mph in 3.2 seconds and to 100 mph in just 7.0 seconds.

FERRARI 599 GTB FIORANO

FERRARI 599 GTB FIORANO
599 GTB

FISKER LATIGO CS

Henrik Fisker's work is well-known, the exterior design of post-2000 Aston Martins being a good example. After leaving Aston, Fisker took up the time-honored craft of coachbuilding. Reviving an art that was prominent before World War II, Fisker starts with an established chassis, removes the bodywork, and affixes his own.

In the case of his Latigo CS, that means beginning with a BMW 6 Series coupe and reskinning it with a Fisker design. Much of this is in advanced materials, with lightweight carbon-fiber/composite for the hood, front and rear fenders, and the trunk lid. The rear spoiler is carbon-fiber. Three-piece forged alloy wheels are wrapped with squat Michelin tires on a lowered sport suspension.

Fisker again starts with the BMW underpinnings for the interior and builds from there. Supple leather is used for the steering wheel, seats, dash panel, center console door panels, and rear side panels. Alcantara goes on the headliner, the side pillars, and parcel shelf. Aluminum shines on the window switch surrounds and iDrive knob.

If Fisker begins with a BMW 650i, you come away with a Latigo urged on by a 4.8-liter V-8 with 360 horsepower, a performance package boosting that to around 470. Base your Latigo CS on BMW's M6 and you get at least 500 horsepower from the 5.0-liter V-10. With the Performance Plus Package, that hikes to 648.

FISKER LATIGO CS

Price: $199,000 (coupe), $204,000 (convertible)
Engine: 360-horsepower, 4.8-liter V-8
0–60 mph: 5.4 seconds
Top speed: 150 mph (electronically limited)

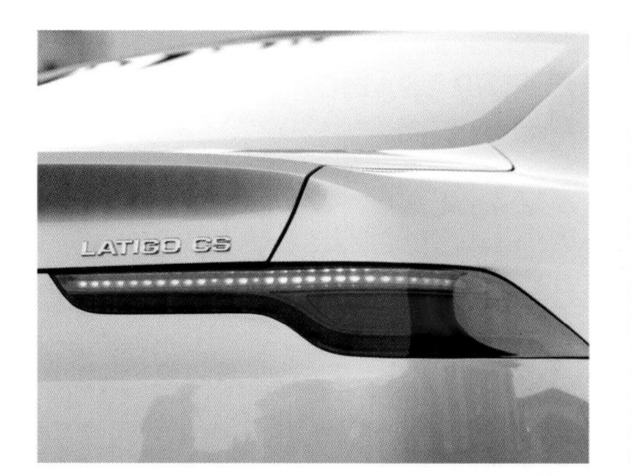

Did You Know?

While the base price of a Fisker Latigo CS coupe is $199,000, you can bump up the cost with little trouble. Opt for the convertible, and you're at $204,000. The V-10 versions begin at $244,000 (coupe) and $249,000 (convertible), while the 648-horsepower editions run to $299,000 for the coupe and $304,000 for the ragtop.

FISKER TRAMONTO

Automotive coachbuilding might be an Italian art, but that didn't stop Henrik Fisker from taking it up in Irvine, California. The Danish-born, ex-BMW, ex-Aston Martin designer hit on the idea of reskinning existing chassis from famous automakers. That would include BMW's 6 Series coupe for the Fisker Latigo CS and Mercedes-Benz's SL sports car under his Tramonto.

Not only is the Mercedes body reshaped, but most of the new panels are done in lightweight carbon-fiber, save for the aluminum doors and steel rear fenders. The suspension is lowered, and the Tramonto glides along on low-profile Michelin tires.

Or roars . . . the more potent variations able to get to 60 mph in the mid-3-second range with a top speed near 200 mph.

Fisker strips out the already-impressive upholstery of the stock SL500 and recovers the seats, steering wheel, interior panels,

FISKER TRAMONTO

Price: $183,500
Engine: 382-horsepower, 5.5-liter V-8
0–60 mph: 5.2 seconds
Top speed: 155 mph (electronically limited)

retractable roll bar, and instrument cluster with upgraded leather. He adds his own graphics to the dials and instruments and redoes many of the switches in aluminum. They even reupholster the inside of the trunk with Alcantara.

Both Mercedes' V-8 and V-12 engines can be used in the Tramonto. Least powerful is the 382-horsepower V-8, though the Fisker/Kleemann-enhanced edition of the AMG supercharged V-8 lifts that to 510 or 590 horsepower. Go with the two-turbo V-12, and you begin with 510 horsepower, then 627. Add the AMG component and the choices are 604 or 700 horsepower.

Did You Know?

The least expensive Fisker is the standard V-8, as they start with a fresh SL500 and ask $183,500 for the finished Fisker. You can work your way through the various V-8 and V-12 permutations right up to the 700-horsepower version at $396,500. However, Fisker will take your old SL500 and make the conversions, "Coachbuild Only" prices ranging from $96,500 to $181,500.

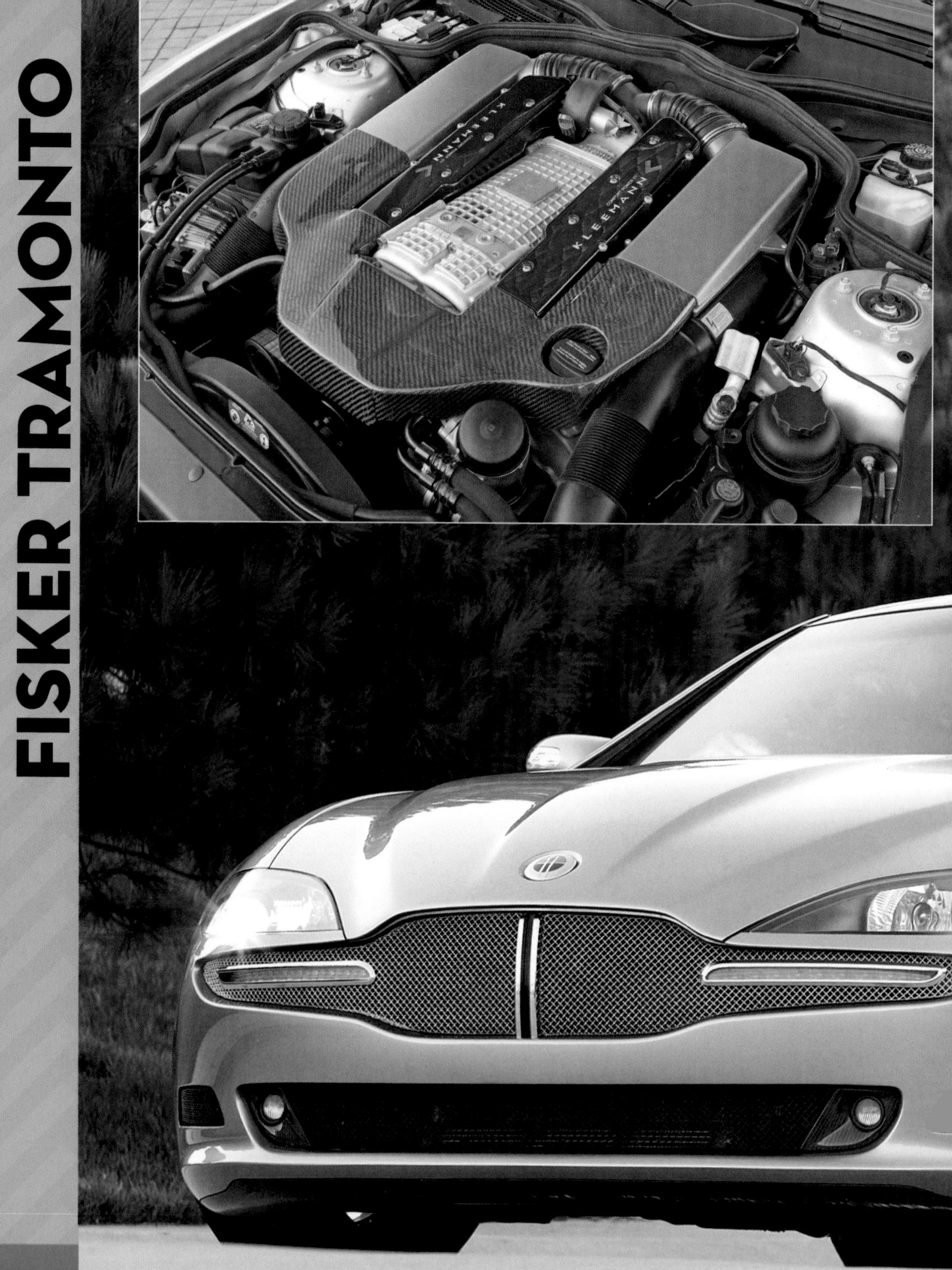
KLEEMANN
KLEEMANN
KLEEMANN

Carroll Shelby and Ford were on the outs for many years. Shelby was off helping with the Dodge Viper and creating his own sports car but eventually linked up with Ford to recreate their classic Shelby Mustang magic.

This time around, the brew gets a supercharger—harkening back to a 1968 Shelby GT350 option—that whomps the 5.4-liter V-8 to 500 horsepower. With the chassis developed by Ford's Special Vehicle Team, you can hustle this Mustang with great speed, even on narrow roads with rough, rumbly surfaces. And when you want to kick forward, just dip into those 500 horses, and the Mustang is gone at a rate that will get you through a quarter-mile in 12.9

FORD SHELBY GT500 & GT500KR

Price: $41,930 (coupe), $46,755 (convertible)
Engine: 500-horsepower, 5.4-liter, supercharged V-8
0–60 mph: 4.5 seconds
Top speed: 155 mph (electronically limited)

seconds at 112 mph.

Ford gave serious attention to the chassis under the 500-horsepower GT500. Suspensions have been firmed and given meaty anti-roll bars. Brembo cross-drilled front brakes measure 14 inches across; the rear discs are from Ford. Tires are P255/45ZR-18 front and P285/40ZR-18 rear.

Dipping into history once again, Carroll Shelby (seen on the next page) and Ford created a modern GT500KR. As in 1968, the "KR" stands for King of the Road. This time it goes for the title with a supercharged, 5.4-liter Ford V-8 with 540 horsepower and 510 lb-ft of torque through a six-speed manual gearbox. Only 1,000 were built.

Did You Know?

Ford was entirely responsible for this Shelby's engine. Based on the company's 5.4-liter V-8, it is capped by an almost evil-looking Eaton Roots–type supercharger. With an intercooler, the blower helps lift horsepower to 500 with the torque at 480 lb-ft, doled out by a six-speed manual transmission.

FORD SHELBY GT500 & GT500KR

GT500KR
40TH

JAGUAR XKR

Jaguar's XK grand touring car got a kick up the performance chart when the British automaker developed its "R" version. You can see the difference as the Jag rushes toward you, the big clue being mesh in the grille and the lower, more aerodynamically efficient, front spoiler. Atop the long hood and along the sides are prominent cooling vents. At the back is a quartet of exhaust pipes. Overall, the XKR has a more aggressive presence.

Pop the hood (the Brit's bonnet), and you'll find the real cause for excitement, a 420-horsepower V-8. To go with the added power are larger front disc brakes and a firmer suspension that improves cornering without a huge degradation in ride.

And standard equipment with any Jaguar sports car is a racetrack heritage that will make any owner proud.

To create the XKR, Jaguar tops its already robust 4.2-liter, aluminum V-8 with an Eaton supercharger. Adding the blower ups horsepower to 420 at 6,000 rpm and torque to 413 lb-ft at 4,000. To this is bolted a six-speed automatic with steering wheel paddle shifters.

Jaguar interiors have long been known for their combination of luxury and sport. Leather upholstery is at the heart of it, and where many Jags in the past have featured wood trim, the XKR goes with aluminum. At the dashboard's center is a touch screen control center that includes navigation.

JAGUAR XKR

Price: $86,035

Engine: 420-horsepower, 4.2-liter, supercharged V-8

0–60 mph: 4.9 seconds

Top speed: 155 mph (electronically limited)

Did You Know?

By adding the supercharger, Jaguar drops its super cat's 0–60 time by more than a second compared to the standard XK, down to 4.9 seconds. The quarter-mile comes up in 12.9 seconds at 110 mph on the way to a top speed that is electronically trimmed to 155 mph.

LEXUS LF-A CONCEPT

Lexus, the luxury division of Toyota, teased us with the LF-A for some time. Design studies were presented at auto shows around the world. Photos of an LF-A prototype had it being tested on the infamous north circuit of Germany's Nürburgring racetrack.

The layout of the LF-A puts the V-10 up front but pulled back into what's called a front mid-engine position. The gearbox is mounted in back as a transaxle. As you can see from the photo of the rear of the car, the radiators are back there too. All this gives the car a good weight distribution to aid handling.

Styling of the LF-A is quite dramatic, a sort of flowing hard-edge feeling we've seen in some past sporty Toyotas. But the shape of the LF-A has to do more than look pretty, as it must help keep the Lexus stable at the car's top speed of 200 mph.

Like BMW's M5 and M6, the LF-A will have a V-10 of some 500 horsepower. And knowing Toyota, the engine will be as well designed and built as the BMW engines. In addition, Lexus has promised a hybrid version of the LF-A, very likely with a system like the Lexus LS 600h sedan, which has a V-8/eletric combo with 438 horsepower.

LEXUS LF-A CONCEPT

Price: est. $150,000
Engine: 500-plus-horsepower, est. 4.9-liter V-10
0–60 mph: est. 3.7 seconds
Top speed: est. 200 mph

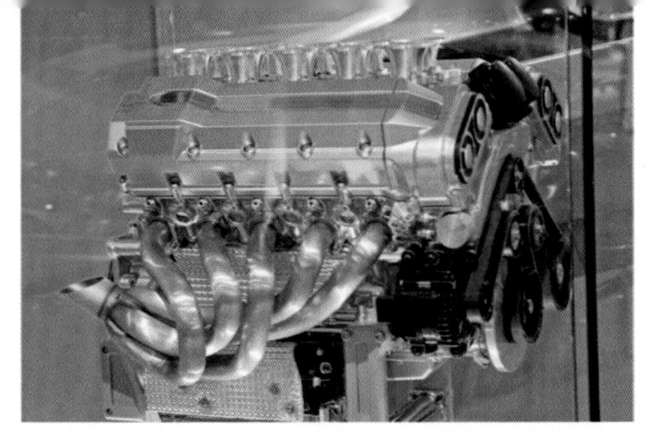

Did You Know?

The design direction of the car is what Lexus calls "LF" for L-Finesse. It's all part of a performance direction for the carmaker, like "AMG" is for Mercedes-Benz and "M" is for BMW.

MASERATI COUPE AND SPYDER

Maserati is one of the proudest exotic automakers in Italy, with a history that combined the talents of six brothers and dates back to the creation of their first car in 1926. In the 1950s, Maserati was a successful rival of Ferrari.

After falling on indifferent times, Maserati came under a Fiat-Ferrari umbrella in 1993. First result of this change was the 1999 3200 GT, which was later joined by a Spyder version. In various forms, the coupe and spyder were built until 2007, when replaced by the GranTurismo.

The first form of the Maserati coupe was called the 3200 GT, which had a 365-horsepower, 3.2-liter, twin-turbo V-6. This was never sold in the United States, and when the Italian automaker decided to sell cars there, it redid the car for 2002 as the Coupe. In went a 390-horsepower V-8 to better suit American tastes.

MASERATI COUPE AND SPYDER

Price: $87,165 (2002 Coupe Cambiocorsa)
Engine: 390-horsepower, 4.2-liter V-8
0–60 mph: 5.0 seconds
Top speed: est. 177 mph

Inside the Coupe is a rather elegant, slightly overstuffed interior that is quite comfortable. It's a generous 2+2 layout, with much of it covered in leather. The detailing is equally well done, right down to the automaker's now-traditional analog clock.

It says "Maserati" on the cam covers, but Ferrari did the V-8 in the Coupe and Spyder. The engine has 90 degrees between cylinder banks, a dry sump oil system, and chain-driven camshafts. That 390 horsepower is joined by 333 lb-ft of torque managed through a six-speed gearbox. A GranSport version has 400 horsepower.

Did You Know?

Giorgetto Giugiaro designed the bodywork, which is certainly handsome, but left many a bit underwhelmed. There was a series of race cars built on the coupe platform and called Trofeo.

MASERATI GRANTURISMO

Maserati got back into the exotic car business with the Coupe, Spyder, and GranSport. Though competent automobiles, the Giugiaro-designed Masers took barbs for being rather conservative looking. To replace the car, Maserati went to Ferrari's long-time design house of preference, Pininfarina. There, Jason Castriota, the young American who also penned Ferrari's 599 GTB Fiorano, created a very exciting shape that borrows from Maserati history but is also quite contemporary.

MASERATI GRANTURISMO

Price: $110,000
Engine: 405-horsepower, 4.2-liter V-8
0–60 mph: 5.2 seconds
Top speed: 177 mph

A Maserati is more than just an exterior design, so the automaker installed a 405-horsepower, Ferrari-built V-8 under the hood and attached it to a ZF six-speed automatic transmission. At the corners are

A-arm independent suspensions and great-looking wheels . . . all in a package that starts around $110,000, like Audi's R8 and Aston Martin's V-8 Vantage.

The grille is pure Maserati, reaching back into the 1950s when the automaker raced head-to-head against cross-town (as in Modena, Italy) rival Ferrari. But those headlamps are modern stuff, as is the chassis under the GranTurismo, which is a shortened form of the platform under Maser's highly regarded Quattroporte super sedan.

One-time Maserati competitor, Ferrari, designed and built the 4.2-liter aluminum V-8 in the GranTurismo's engine bay. It brings not only 405 horsepower, but also great tradition and a healthy exhaust note.

Did You Know?

Half the fun of having an exotic car is its interior, and Maserati's GranTurismo doesn't disappoint. There's leather everywhere, it seems, and you can see the tight stitching on the comfy-but-supportive seats. Again, it's a combo of tradition, like the classic white-on-black gauges and a high-tech navigational system.

MASERATI GRANTURISMO

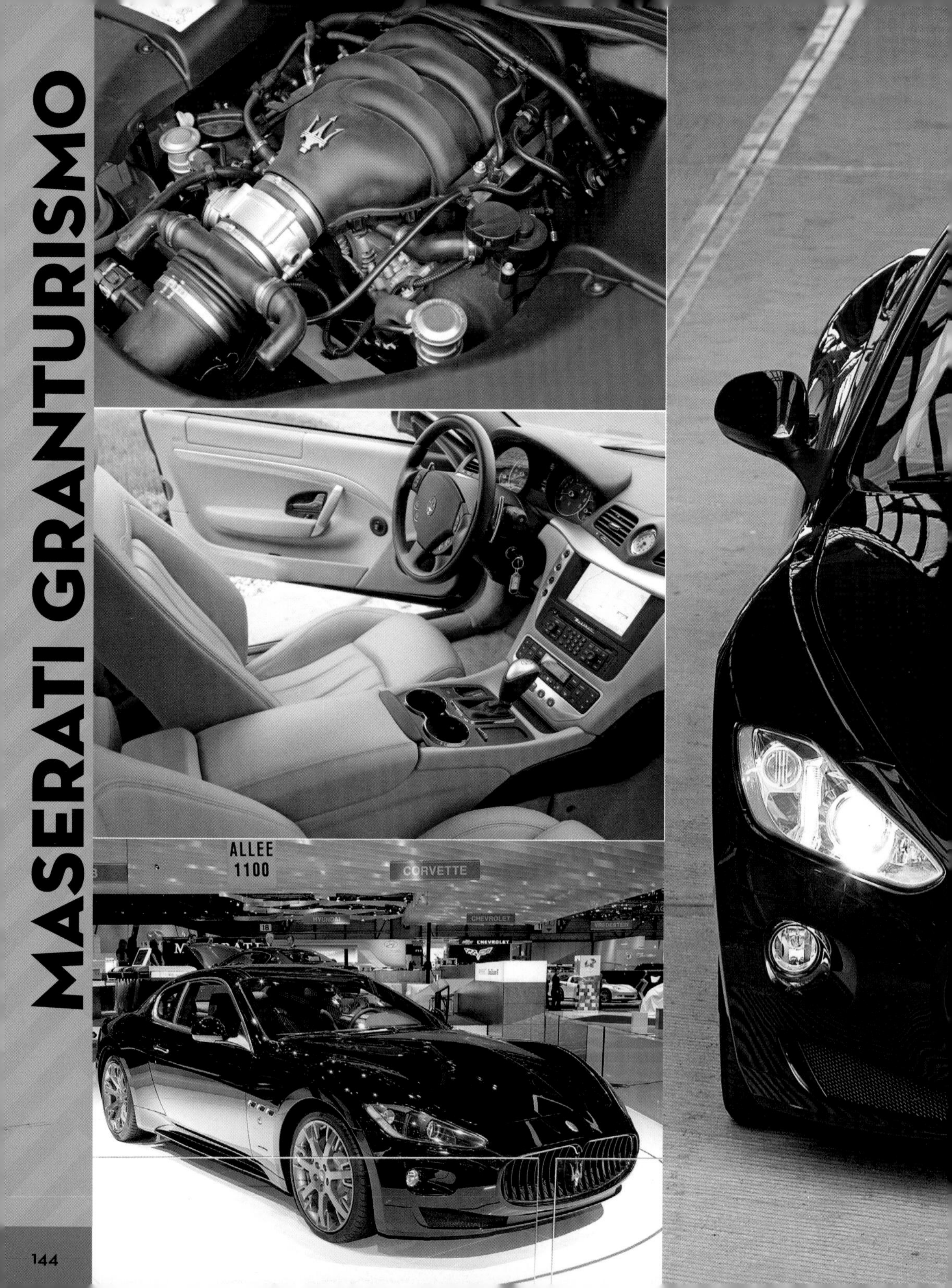

MASERATI GRANTURISMO

With its long nose, the SLR has somewhat controversial styling, though it undoubtedly has a dramatic-looking long-hood, short-deck proportion. That shape is done in carbon-fiber-reinforced plastic, the drivetrain bolted to a pair of aluminum frames. Naturally, the shape was fine-tuned in the wind tunnel with a sealed underbody tray and a flip-up spoiler at the rear.

The suspension is a race-tuned independent design, the brakes featuring huge carbon-ceramic discs that can stop the car from its 200-plus-mph top speed repeatedly with no fade.

MERCEDES-BENZ SLR

Price: $450,000
Engine: 617-horsepower, 5.4-liter, supercharged V-8
0–60 mph: 3.5 seconds
Top speed: 207 mph

To power the SLR, Mercedes went to its AMG subsidiary for a hand-built, 5.4-liter, supercharged aluminum V-8. With 13 psi of boost from its Lysholm-type supercharger, the engine dynos at 617 horsepower and 575

lb-ft of torque. The transmission is a five-speed with two fully automatic modes, plus a paddle shifter manual phase with three modes of its own.

As with Mercedes' classic 300SL from the early 1950s, the SLR has swing-up doors. This is the 722 Edition launched in 2006, the horsepower increased to 650 and torque to 605 lb-ft. The body is lowered 0.4 inch, the suspension is stiffened, and the 722 rides on unique 19.0-inch wheels.

At the 2007 Frankfurt Auto Show, Mercedes had the world premier of the roadster version of the SLR. The fabric top can be had in any of three colors, and you lower it simply by unlatching it from the windshield frame and slightly raising it. In 10 seconds, it's folded flat and covered by an aluminum cover.

Did You Know?

Mercedes-Benz and its Grand Prix partner, McLaren, combined to create the front-engine SLR supercar. Launched in 2003, Mercedes said it would build only 3,500 in a factory shared with McLaren in Woking, England.

SLR
premiere.
McLaren
H دبي DUBAI 01 2008 97243

MERCEDES-BENZ CL65 AMG

Imagine this: You pull up to a stoplight next to a guy in a hot Mustang with a growly exhaust. You are in a big Mercedes coupe, and he assumes you're a luxury guy with no sense of speed. Light turns green, and you smoke him with your big Merc. If the road is right, you could nail down a trip to 60 mph in just 4.2 seconds.

For all its luxury, Mercedes loves to do this with all its models, the CL coupe being no exception. Check out the two-bar front grille and gnarly front spoiler. Under that sloped hood is a 604-horsepower, twin-turbo V-12.

You cannot consecrate a supercar with 738 lb-ft of torque and not also appropriately bless the suspension. For the CL65, AMG adds huge cross-drilled disc brakes, the fronts with what are called twin sliding calipers. The 20-inch tires measure 235/35 at the front and 275/35 to the rear, while the suspension is firmed with special AMG spring struts.

The wizards at AMG in Affalterbach, Germany, have been working their magic on Mercedes-Benz engines for 40 years. For the CL65 AMGs they hand-build the 6.0-liter V-12s—the builder's signature atop each engine—by adding a pair of turbochargers and taking power to 604 horsepower and, even more impressive, boosting torque to 738 lb-ft.

MERCEDES-BENZ CL65 AMG

Price: $197,000 (2008)
Engine: 604-horsepower, 6.0-liter, twin-turbo V-12
0–60 mph: 4.2 seconds
Top speed: 155 mph (electronically limited)

Did You Know?

A rare bird, this is one of only 40 anniversary edition CL65 AMGs, the clue being the rather amazing AMG Alubeam Liquid Metal paint. Price tag? Just $197,000, which would buy a lot of Mustangs.

MERCEDES-BENZ CL65 AMG

MERCEDES-BENZ C63 AMG

Mercedes-Benz has long had a pumped-up version of its small sedan, but BMW has owned the hearts and minds of the small German performance market with the M3. This finally got Mercedes ticked-off, because with its latest "AMG-ized" C-Class, it goes hammers and tongs after the Bimmer.

You see it first on the nose of the C63 AMG, which is significantly more in BMW's face with an aggressive front redesign. Work your way back along the fender flares, from the new sill panels to the rear lip spoiler, and it's obvious this Mercedes means business.

MERCEDES-BENZ C63 AMG

Price: est. $63,000
Engine: 450-horsepower, 6.2-liter V-8
0–60 mph: 4.5 seconds
Top speed: 174 mph (with optional Performance Package)

AMG's business is speed, and that comes from a 6.2-liter, hand-built V-8 with 450 horsepower and 443 lb-ft of torque handled by a seven-speed paddle 7G Tronic automatic that pops shifts right there with the quicker

semi-automatics.

Not only does it look powerful with its crisscross intake runners, but the AMG V-8's dual exhausts have a snappy basso profundo note. You hear it under hard acceleration and when the transmission blips the V-8's throttle on downshifts.

In the C63's cockpit, you see much of the standard C-Class with AMG spiffs, like its specific gauges and sport seats. From the driver's seat, you can easily snap the car through its 0–60 paces, but the most fun is when you ease it quickly through corners and feel the AMG corner so securely.

Did You Know?

With the AMG V-8 some 4 inches longer than the V-6 normally used in the C-Class, Mercedes designed a new nose for the C63 that's 3.4 inches longer than the stock machine. Note the little power domes on the hood and the car's athletic stance on the road.

MERCEDES-BENZ C63 AMG

CEDES-BENZ C63 AMG
K 6329

Driving a Grand Prix car on the street would be highly impractical, but you can come close to using Formula 1's official track safety car on public roads. That would be the Mercedes-Benz CLK65 AMG Black Series, a lightweight, high-powered, flared carbon fiber–fender version of its tamer CLK road car.

MERCEDES-BENZ CLK65 AMG BLACK SERIES

Price: $135,000
Engine: 507-horsepower, 6.2-liter V-8
0–60 mph: 4.1 seconds
Top speed: 186 mph (electronically limited)

The Black Series looks nicely nasty, sitting low, with very aggressive nose and rear spoilers. Performance items include a limited-slip differential and an oil cooler for the rear differential.

While some exotic cars would leave your hearing dulled and your backside numbed after even a short drive, the Black Series

is surprisingly civilized considering its potential. In fact, the suspension can be adjusted for road or track performance, making this a true dual-personality machine.

The interior might be called semi-race car. There is no back seat, and the front pair are racing types covered in nappa leather that hold you firmly. There's plenty of carbon-fiber in view and a small steering wheel with aluminum shift paddles that allow you to pop shifts in either a Sport or Manual mode. The suspension is firm, but not overly so, providing not just superb handling but a reasonably supple ride.

Normally, AMG modifies Mercedes engines, but for the Black Series CLK the tuning firm designed a powerful V-8. Sharing no parts with Mercedes' engines, the powerplant is not supercharged and yet gets 507 horsepower and 464 lb-ft of torque from its 6.2 liters. The gearbox is a seven-speed paddle-shifted automatic.

Did You Know?

To keep weight low, those front fenders, like several body parts on the Black Series CLK, are made of carbon-fiber. The wheels are from AMG, forged in aluminum and fitted with low-aspect-ratio Pirelli P Zero tires.

CLK 63

This might sound a bit insulting to those who are used to ground-pounding supercars, but Mercedes-Benz SLs are sweethearts. Why that description? It's used to denote most any car that is the sum total of a near-perfect design. Whether you're considering its visual appearance, interior, performance, or ride and handling, the SL just shines.

For 2009, Mercedes has reworked much of the exterior of the SL, particularly the front. A new single-bar grille is more aggressive, as are larger front air intakes and a pair of power domes on the hood. Out back is an air diffuser in the bumper.

In a mere 16 seconds the open SL will convert into a well-sealed coupe. In addition to a beautifully upholstered interior, driver and passenger get a roll bar that pops up in case of an accident. Hopefully of more use is the Airscarf. This is in each seat headrest and blows warm air on the necks of driver and passenger when things get a bit chilly.

Engines in the SLs come in four flavors. SL550s get a 382-horsepower 5.5-liter V-8 (seen here) and SL63s a 518-horsepower 6.2-liter V-8 backed by a seven-speed automatic transmission. The SL600 and SL65 are equipped with V-12s and five-speed automatics that match their, respectively, 510 horsepower and 604 horsepower . . . the latter doing 0–60 mph in 4.2 seconds.

MERCEDES-BENZ SL

Price: $132,125
Engine: 518-horsepower, 6.2-liter V-8
0–60 mph: 4.7 seconds
Top speed: 186 mph (with special performance option)

Did You Know?

Available with V-8 or V-12 engines, the SL can be had as merely a powerful cruiser or a flat-out (though still luxurious) hot rod.

NISSAN SKYLINE GT-R

Many Americans know little of Nissan's Skylines, but in Japan and Europe they are legendary. The all-wheel-drive cars have a great racing history, even being banned from a few series in Europe because they were so fast.

Now Nissan is at last bringing the latest Skyline GT-R to the United States. The exterior design is very aggressive, a great mix of guts and muscle that gets right in your face. And the GT-R has the performance to back up its looks, the sort that will have Skyline owners worrying the likes of Porsche and Ferrari drivers.

NISSAN SKYLINE GT-R
Price: est. $70,000
Engine: 480-horsepower, twin-turbo V-6
0–60 mph: 3.5 seconds
Top speed: 190 mph

Skylines are famous for their six-cylinder engines, a 3.8-liter V-6 in the GT-R. Each engine is hand-built, with a turbo for each side, whooshing it to 480 horsepower and 430 lb-ft of torque. Paired with the V-6 is a

six-speed transmission shifted via steering wheel–mounted paddles.

GT-Rs lay their impressive power down through Nissan's ATTESA E-TS all-wheel, which electronically doles out the 480 horsepower as it can best be used. The independent suspension has years of racing experience designed into it. The new GT-R proved this by rushing around the famed Nürburgring in Germany in 7:38, a heroic time for a production car.

Many of those in the United States who know the Skyline have driven it . . . in video games, where it is a favorite. So it isn't surprising there's a bit of video game in the instrumentation. Still, the GT-R is usable as a daily driver, with generous coupe accommodations and room in the trunk for a pair of golf bags.

Did You Know?

These high-performance machines have been around for four decades, endorsed long ago by none other than Paul Newman.

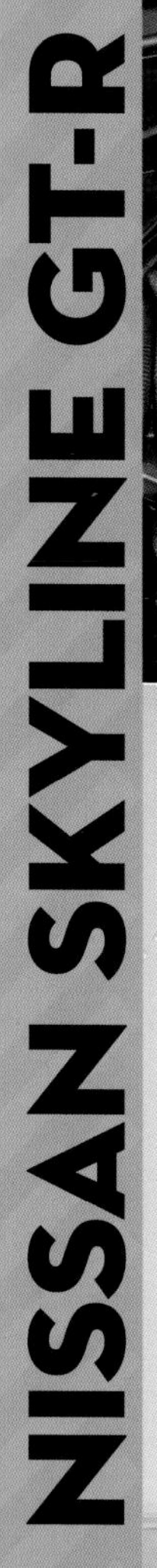
NISSAN SKYLINE GT-R

NISSAN

SALEEN MUSTANG S281

Steve Saleen began modifying Mustangs years ago, initially to go racing. He was quite successful at this, winning a number of Sports Car Club of America championships. He formed a partnership with comedian Tim Allen and successes continued, leading to the development of the mid-engine Saleen S7 supercar and then the manufacture of the Ford GT for Ford.

But the business has never forgotten its Mustang roots, as one can see in the S281. Hand-assembled in Irvine, California, Saleen Mustangs offer great performance for the money. Not that they are cheap. It isn't difficult to drop $50,000 on a standard S281 coupe, while a well-equipped S281 Extreme can go to $80,000. If you want to have some fun, sign on to www.saleen.com and spec out your own S281.

SALEEN MUSTANG S281

Price: $59,015 (Parnelli Jones special edition)
Engine: 400-horsepower, 4.9-liter V-8
0–60 mph: 4.7 seconds
Top speed: est. 145 mph

Saleen reworks both Mustang coupes and convertibles. As you can see, it isn't just the engine and suspension that get the works. New front spoilers, hoods, sills, rear spoilers, and, of course, wheels are all part of the package.

Saleen Mustangs are called S281s, and the 4.9-liter V-8 can be tuned to three levels of power. The "normal" S281 dynos at 335 horsepower and 345 lb-ft of torque. Step up to the supercharged/intercooled version seen here, and you're talking 465 horsepower and 425 lb-ft of torque. But wait, there's more: the S281 Extreme at 550 horsepower and 525 lb-ft of torque.

Did You Know?

Saleen also performs its tricks on Ford's F150 pickup trucks, from the two-passenger to the Supercrew versions. Called an S331, you can get it with the 24-valve, 325-horsepower, 5.6-liter V-8 with 380 lb-ft of torque or they will supercharge it to 450 horsepower and 500 lb-ft of torque. Hold on tight!

2005
SALEEN

SALEEN MUSTANG S281

CHAPTER 3

MID-ENGINE ATTRA

TION

The last Formula 1 race won by a front-engine machine was American Phil Hill's Ferrari victory in the 1960 Italian Grand Prix. By the mid-1960s, the change to mid-engines was underway in sports car racing and at the United States' most important race, the Indianapolis 500.

Come 1966, Lamborghini launched the mid-engine production Miura, and this layout became the design of choice for truly exotic street machines. Enzo Ferrari, always rather conservative, held out against the trend, but the mid-engine V-6 Dino and then the flat 12 Berlinetta Boxer marked his conversion to mid-engine.

There are several advantages to this layout in an exotic, though the main one is weight distribution and handling. And there are disadvantages, like packaging.

While a mid-engine design works nicely in a machine with a V-8 or small V-10 engine—cars like the Ferrari F430, Lamborghini Gallardo, or Audi R8—those with big rear powerplants can get a bit big in the backside, making them bulky and unwieldy for daily use. This explains why Ferrari abandoned the mid-engine layout for its big car after the demise of the Testarossa in 1996 but retains it for the F430.

There has long been one exception to this trend: Porsche. From its humble Volkswagen beginnings, the German sports car maker has always used a rear engine, back behind the rear axle. Still, the fine handling qualities of the current 911s are a triumph of engineering over basic principles. For years, 911s had questionable handling, and even Porsche was in the forefront of the swing to mid-engines with its co-design of the 914 with VW, debuted in September 1969. As the German firm has introduced new sports car models in recent years—the Boxster, Carrera GT, and Cayman—all have mid-engine configurations.

The reality is that modern engineering advances, from traction control to yaw-control suspension devices, have made the inherent handling advantages of a mid-engine layout less of a factor.

Still, there's something about the shape and stance of a great mid-engine exotic car that is undeniably exciting.

Stirs the soul, doesn't it?

ACURA NSX

It can be argued that owners of all modern exotic cars should say thanks to the Acura NSX designers and engineers and the car's executive chief engineer, Shigeru Uehara. When the mid-engine Honda-made sports car came along in 1991, it seriously upped the quality ante for anyone who cared to sell an exotic machine.

Not only was the Honda good-looking—thanks to Pininfarina and Ken Okuyama, who later designed the Enzo—but it was as reliable as, well, a Honda.

You'll read how Ferrari extols the aluminum chassis and bodies of its modern cars, and well it should. But Honda was there first with the NSX. And with a rich Formula 1 history, the drivetrain of this now classic sports car is jewel-like and rugged. Just as you'd expect from a Honda.

ACURA NSX

Price: $89,000 (2005)

Engine: 290-horsepower, 3.2-liter V-6

0–60 mph: 4.9 seconds

Top speed: 175 mph

Aluminum was the key to the light weight of the NSX. The metal was used for the chassis, the body, the suspension A-arms and hubs, the road wheels, and much of the drivetrain, though even-lighter titanium was used for the connecting rods.

By the end of its lifespan in 2005, the NSX was offered with two versions of its Formula 1–inspired V-6. If you were a manual gearbox fan, you'd opt for the 3.2-liter edition with 290 horsepower, 224 lb-ft of torque, and six speeds. Prefer an automatic? Then you'd get a 3.0-liter V-6 with 252 horsepower, 210 lb-ft of torque, and four speeds. There is a great sense of rushing over the road when you drive an NSX, and if you're a fresh air fan, the targa roof can be removed.

Did You Know?

Honda said the interior of the NSX was inspired by jet fighter cockpits, with supportive seats, dials that are easy to read, and excellent visibility.

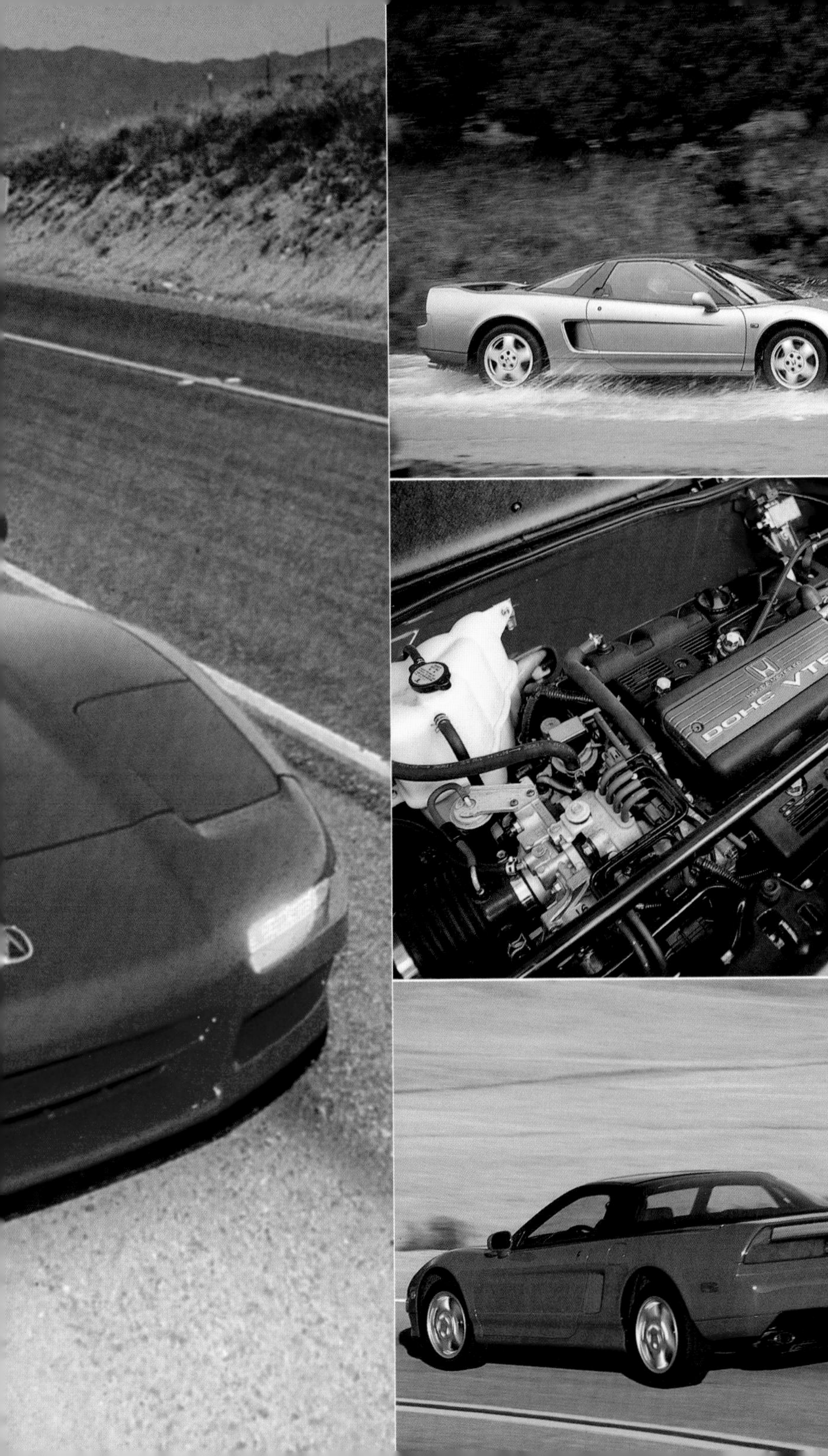
DOHC VTEC

Even though it owns Lamborghini, Audi wanted its own mid-engine exotic car, hence the R8. Perhaps it was the inspiration of its mighty Le Mans–winning machines that spurred on the German manufacturer, but whatever led to the R8 worked.

Okay, $110,000 is still costly, but what you get is worth the price—that somewhat avant-garde exterior design with its slightly evil-looking headlamps and the aggressive side profile. And though the silver "side blade" can be a bit controversial, you can order it in body color or carbon-fiber. Even going away, the R8 looks exotic and businesslike.

And what a drivetrain, 420 strong horsepower put on the road through all-wheel drive and a finely tuned suspension, the mid-engine layout making this one delightfully balanced machine.

AUDI R8
Price: $110,000
Engine: 420-horsepower, 4.2-liter V-8
0–60 mph: 4.3 seconds
Top speed: 187 mph

Driving the R8 is a treat, whether trundling quietly thought the streets of Miami or carving up a mountain road in Colorado. The interior is quite comfortable but also highly functional, from it D-shaped steering wheel to its tap-the-next-gear paddle shifters to excellent down-the-road visibility.

Suspensions for the R8 have upper and lower A-arms, coil springs, and electronically adjustable shocks, the trick being to add Audi's optional Magnetic Ride for an impressive combination of ride and handling. Brakes are 15.0-inch discs in front, with 14.0-inch discs at the back.

Did You Know?

The R8 borrows its V-8 from Audi's RS 4, and that's a good thing. With a displacement of 4.2 liters, the lightweight aluminum V-8 provides 420 horsepower and 317 lb-ft of torque between 4,500 and 6,000 rpm. Best gearbox? The traditional six-speed manual.

V8 FSI

MICHIGAN
006M303

BUGATTI EB110

Name the most important men in automobiles, and the list usually includes Henry Ford, Enzo Ferrari, Soichiro Honda, and Ettore Bugatti. Most people know the first three, but who was Bugatti? In the 1920s and 1930s, this artist–engineer created a series of truly magnificent automobiles, from small Grand Prix machines to huge touring cars.

The Bugatti magic was such that many have tried to re-create it, the most recent being Volkswagen. But in the late 1980s and early 1990s, a man called Romano Artioli tried to revive the marque with the mid-engine EB110. Built in Campogalliano, Italy, near Ferrari, Lamborghini, and Maserati, the EB110 was impressive for its power and driving qualities. But the EB110 suffered bad timing, and the company built at most 150 cars before bankruptcy.

BUGATTI EB110

Price: $350,000
Engine: 560-horsepower, 3.5-liter, quad-turbo V-12
0–60 mph: 3.3 seconds
Top speed: 217 mph

Marcello Gandini, designer of the Lamborghini Countach, was contracted to pen the exterior of the EB110. The rear view isn't inspiring, but seen from the front with the small traditional Bugatti horseshoe grille or from the front three-quarter view, the shape is impressive.

It's quite luxurious inside an EB110, past its flip-up Lamborghini-style doors. The seats look more like lounge chairs than racer's seats. It's very much a driver's car, the gauges all captured in a display encapsulated for the pilot.

Did You Know?

Paolo Stanzani of Lamborghini fame gets credit for the EB110's impressive engine. The V-12 has only 3.5 liters, but with four turbochargers and 560 horsepower. This power goes back through a custom-made gearbox and into an all-wheel-drive system for maximum traction.

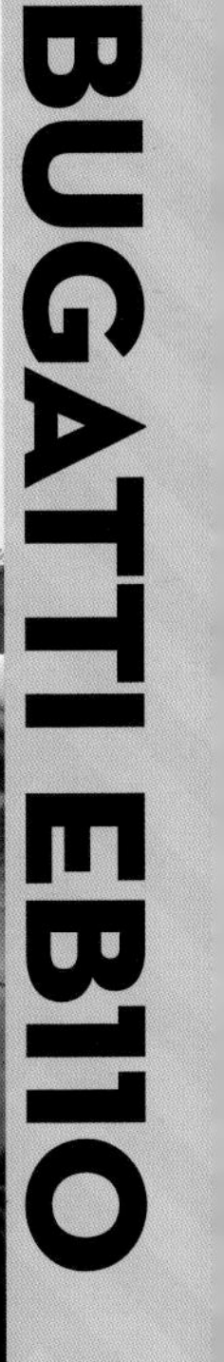

BUGATTI VEYRON 16.4

So, what do you want for your $1.5 million?

In the case of the Bugatti Veyron, it would be a stunning exterior design that not only makes a strong styling statement but also helps the car to its 253-mph top speed.

How about an engine with the rare "W" configuration and 1,001 horsepower? Just as impressive when you drive the Bugatti is its seven-speed, twin-clutch, automatic transmission that zings you from gear to gear at fraction-of-a-blink speeds through all-wheel drive.

BUGATTI VEYRON 16.4

Price: $1,500,000
Engine: 1,001-horsepower, 8.0-liter, quad-turbo W-16
0–60 mph: 2.6 seconds
Top speed: 253 mph

Then there's an interior that is simply splendid with its acres of leather and fine detailing.

And it's a Volkswagen. At least, the German company is the parent of this

modern reincarnation of the firm run before World War II by the legendary Ettore Bugatti.

Having no engine cover leaves the W-16 out in plain view and aids cooling. This amazing powerplant has 16 cylinders in the unusual "W" layout, four turbochargers, and 8.0 liters of displacement. Not only does it have 1,001 horsepower but 922 lb-ft of torque, launching the 4,470-pound supercar to 60 mph in 2.6 seconds.

You won't hear many people call the Veyron beautiful, but no one denies that it has an exciting exterior shape. Up front is the traditional horseshoe-shaped grille that has been a part of every Bugatti. Out back is the tall spoiler needed to stabilize the car at speed.

Did You Know?

Fine leather covers most surfaces, the others having an engine-turned surface that was popular with Ettore Bugatti. The interior is a fine place to be, though the low roof does give a slight "bunker effect" to the cockpit.

BUGATTI VEYRON 16.4

3258 W 67

BUGATTI VEYRON 16.4

"For of all sad words of tongue or pen, the saddest are these: 'It might have been.'"

Having died in 1892, John Greenleaf Whittier couldn't have been referring to Chrysler's ME Four-Twelve concept when he wrote those famous words, but they fit.

During the brightest years of the soon-to-dim Chrysler-Daimler alliance, the two automakers mixed and matched parts, and one result was this great supercar concept. Maybe it was the idea of Ford doing the GT or German rival VW's Bugatti Veyron, but at the 2004 Detroit Auto Show, Chrysler unveiled the ME Four-Twelve. The name refers to the layout, *M*id-*E*ngine with *Four* turbos on the AMG *Twelve*-cylinder engine.

Chrysler showed a fully running prototype and even gave the press rides, but the business case was tough and then came the divorce. No ME Four-Twelve.

How sad.

Lurking under that rear engine cover is the German side of the equation, a 6.0-liter AMG V-12 with four turbochargers, a reported 850 horsepower, and a stunning 850 lb-ft of torque. Ricardo did the seven-speed dual-clutch transmission, the same type it designed for Bugatti's Veyron.

This is what made the ME Four-Twelve seem so promising, a running prototype of the mid-engine Chrysler in the flat black of its carbon-fiber bodywork. The monocoque tub was of carbon-fiber and aluminum honeycomb, and the suspension was based on A-arms, with the brake discs made of carbon ceramic.

CHRYSLER ME FOUR-TWELVE CONCEPT

Price: Not Applicable
Engine: 850-horsepower, 6.0-liter, quad-turbo V-12
0–60 mph: est. 2.9 seconds
Top speed: est. 249 mph

Did You Know?

Its drivetrain may have been German, but the exterior design was all-American. The nose is decidedly Chrysler and the overall shape dramatic, while the interior is a mix of materials, chrome-rimmed gauges, and controls with lighting that has a hint of jukebox.

FERRARI 360 MODENA

By 1999, it was time to replace the F355, which had been a development of the 348. This time, Ferrari completely redesigned its mid-engine V-8 sports car. Working with Alcoa, the Italian automaker designed an all-aluminum space frame chassis that is wrapped in aluminum bodywork. Though 28 percent lighter than the F355 and a bit larger, the aluminum chassis is 40 percent stiffer. The resulting car is quite good, particularly the Spider version, which is solid even on rough roads.

This time, Ferrari's V-8 sports car had the F131 V-8 with 3.6 liters—hence the 360 in the name—Modena being the site of Enzo Ferrari's original factory. In the 360 coupe and Spider, the engine promised 395 horsepower and 275 lb-ft of torque. For the faster Challenge Stradale version,

FERRARI 360 MODENA

Price: $146,930

Engine: 395-horsepower, 3.6-liter V-8

0–60 mph: 4.3 seconds

Top speed: 189 mph

horsepower went to 425, though torque was unchanged.

As it has since the mid-1950s, Pininfarina created the shape of the 360. The front didn't get the greatest reviews, but the overall form is quite nice, particularly with the Spider. In the coupe, the engine cover is done in glass.

Ferrari's classic sort of interior continued, including great seats, instantly legible instrumentation, and all controls right at hand. That would include the paddle shifters at the steering wheel for the F1 system, an option to the normal six-speed manual. At this point, the system worked nicely if manually shifted but was balky in its "automatic" mode.

Did You Know?

In 2003, Ferrari introduced the Challenge Stradale version of the 360, cutting some 50 pounds, upping horsepower by 30, and adding carbon-ceramic brakes. Ferrari also built a lineup of 360 Challenge cars that raced in a one-marque series.

Ferrari

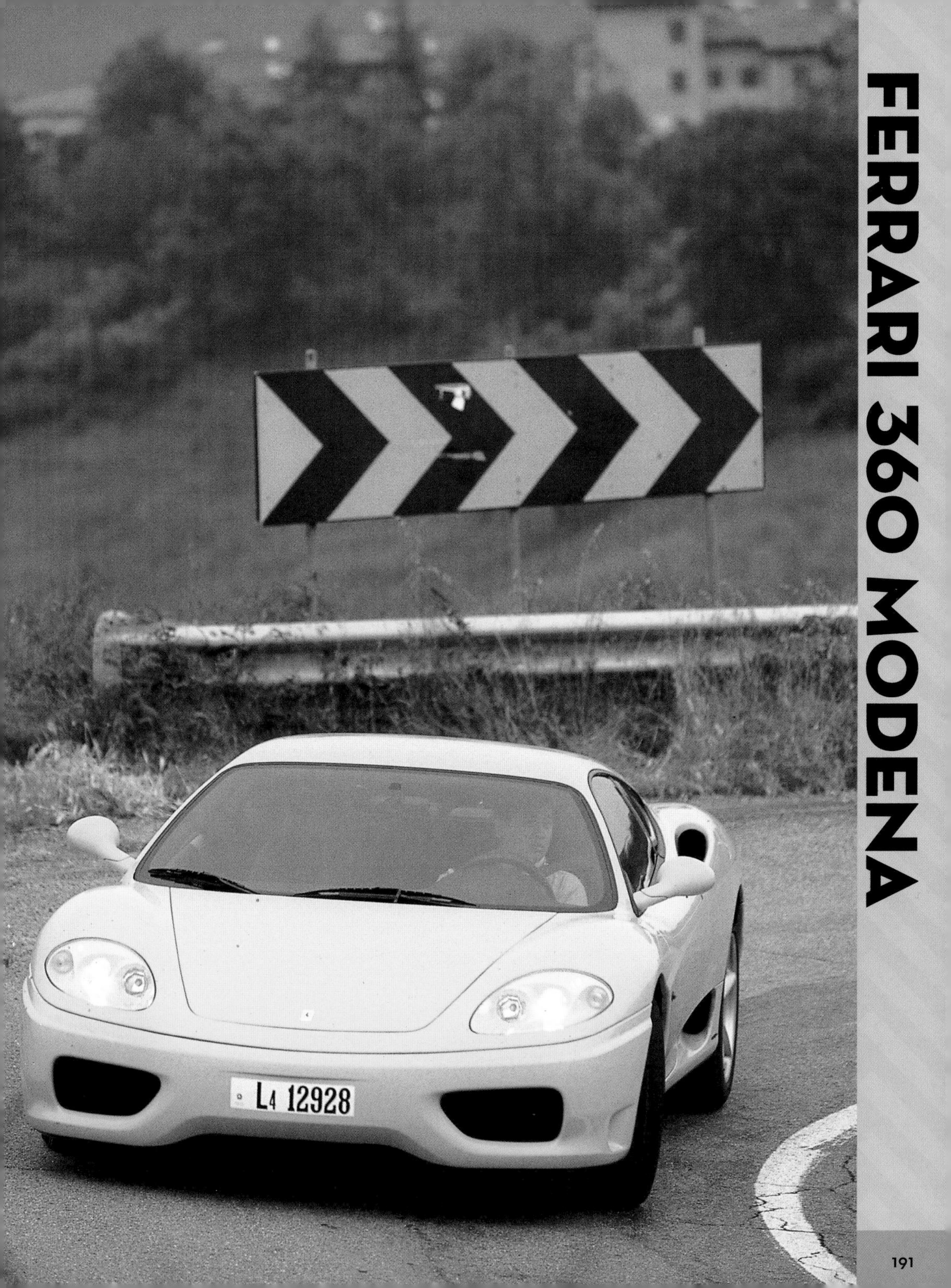

FERRARI 360 MODENA

FERRARI F430

There are quite a few excellent mid-engine supercars, but to many experts, the best of the bunch is Ferrari's F430. It begins with the Pininfarina styling, the twin-snout front end quite reminiscent of the front of the Grand Prix machine of U.S. Formula 1 champion Phil Hill.

FERRARI F430

Price: $173,079 (coupe), $201,213 (spider)
Engine: 483-horsepower, 4.3-liter V-8
0–60 mph: 3.5 seconds
Top speed: 198 mph

Inside is a mixture of leather and carbon-fiber in a design that balances luxury with hard-driving sportiness. Out back is a 4.3-liter V-8 that boasts 483 horsepower and 343 lb-ft of torque. The most intriguing component is the F1, paddle-shifted, six-speed transmission with its lightning-quick shifts.

What is really appealing, however, is the manner in which all the F430's parts and

pieces are assembled in an automobile that is just as willing to trundle through town as to cut hot laps on a racetrack.

Ferrari's famous steering wheel has its red "START" button on the left and the *manettino* on the right. With this latter switch, you can vary the handling characteristics of the F430, along with how the F1 transmission shifts. You can see the left-side shift paddle just ahead of the steering wheel.

You can have the standard four-wheel disc brakes or pop in an extra $15,000 for the carbon ceramics. Though pricey, these brakes not only shorten braking distances, but also have virtually no fade. The tires are low-profile Pirelli Potenzas on aluminum

Did You Know?

Ferrari uses the F430 for its Ferrari Challenge Series. Though it looks like the standard car, it is all race under the skin, from the liberal use of carbon-fiber for lower weight to a full roll cage. All cars use factory-sealed 479-horsepower V-8s.

FERRARI F430

MOTOROLA
Sabelt
Sabelt
GRAND AM
PIRELLI
PIRELLI

FERRARI F430
ENGINE START

FERRARI 430 SCUDERIA

After Ferrari establishes a mid-engine V-8 sports car, it likes to create a super version. From the 360 Modena, Ferrari developed the 360 Stradale, while the F430 is the basis for the 430 Scuderia.

Weight is down, horsepower is up, and the Scuderia scrambles to 60 in 3.5 seconds but the true development is in the suspension. The further-refined design is said to help get the Scuderia around Ferrari's Fiorano test track faster than the legendary Enzo. And just as the Enzo proved to be a surprisingly civilized machine to drive every day, so too the Scuderia achieves its level of handling competence without any great sacrifice in ride quality.

There's a distinct race car feeling to the interior of the 430 Scuderia. Part of that comes from the functional feeling of the instrumentation. Then there are the seats, contoured to hold driver and passenger in place during hard driving. And Ferrari stripped much of the interior trim.

Ferrari cut the F430's weight by 220 pounds for the 430 Scuderia. Among other things, the use of carbon-fiber increased, the engine seeming to be in a sea of it. With the increased horsepower and lower weight, the Ferrari's top speed is just a touch shy of 200 miles per hour.

FERRARI 430 SCUDERIA

Price: est. $250,000

Engine: 510-horsepower, 4.3-liter V-8

0–60 mph: 3.5 seconds

Top speed: 198 mph

Did You Know?

At the business end of the 430 Scuderia, Ferrari has upped the horsepower from 490 to 510. Torque is at 347 lb-ft on a fat torque curve. Banging through the paddle-shifted six-speed you can get the Ferrari to 60 mph in 3.5 seconds.

FERRARI ENZO

Following in the tire tracks of its F40 and F50 supercars, Ferrari created the Enzo in 2002 as proof of the company's technical prowess. The car's edgy Pininfarina carbon-fiber bodywork certainly makes a statement. Under that skin is still more of the lightweight carbon-fiber combined with honeycomb aluminum panels to create a central tub weighing a mere 202 pounds.

Other chassis components include upper and lower A-arm suspensions and lightweight, extremely powerful, carbon-ceramic brakes.

FERRARI ENZO

Price: $652,830
Engine: 650-horsepower, 6.0-liter V-12
0–60 mph: 3.3 seconds
Top speed: 217 mph

Not only does the Enzo get to 60 in 3.3 seconds, but it then gobbles up the quarter-mile in 11.1 seconds at 133 mph.

Enzo designer Ken Okuyama (then with Pininfarina) says of the car's shape, "In the Enzo's case, we really wanted to make a

statement for the decades." And they did that with the stirring but controversial shape of the Ferrari, which is capable of 217 mph without the need for external wings.

This is another of the great Ferrari supercars powered by a V-12, here filling out at 6.0 liters, with 48 valves, 650 horsepower, and 485 lb-ft of torque. Getting that power to the ground is a six-speed, paddle-actuated transmission.

Step in, ease down into those carbon-fiber–shell seats, and it feels a bit like the Enzo is giving you a hug around the middle. Red leather and carbon-fiber are the main themes inside the super-quick Ferrari, which is deceptively easy to drive.

Did You Know?

Ferrari said it would build 399 Enzos but then broke that promise by one, though for a good cause. The 400th Enzo was given to the Pope and was then auctioned off for charity.

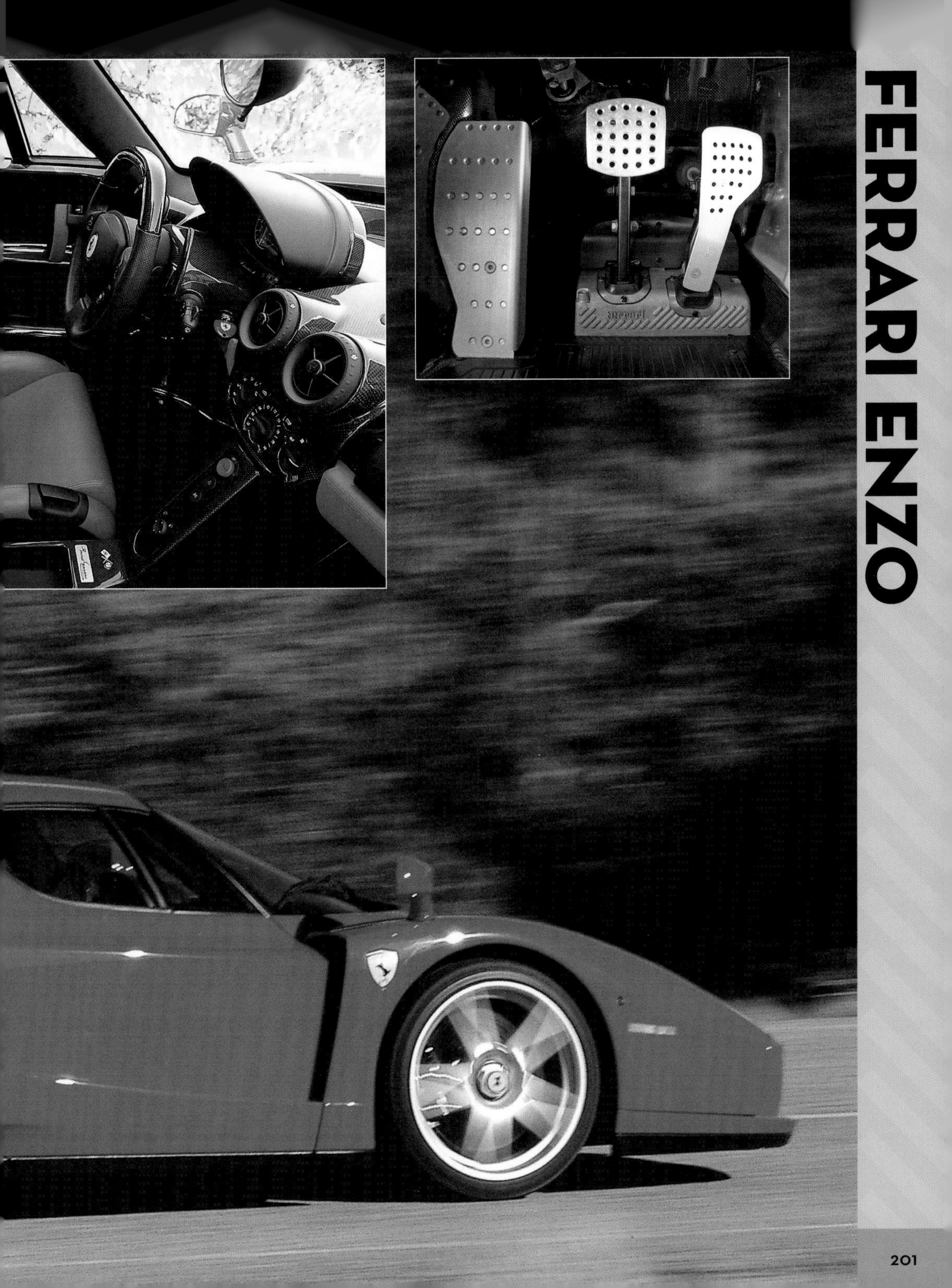

After Ferrari built its announced 400 Enzos, the same carbon-fiber tub was used for the Maserati MC12. End of the line for the design? No, because then Ferrari announced the FXX.

This wasn't your usual buy-it-and-drive-it program, Ferrari pointing out that the FXX is homologated for neither road nor track. Instead, for your $1.9 million you got the car and the chance to use it at Ferrari-sponsored race days. Ferrari would monitor the sessions and use the information for future Ferrari automobiles. You had to be an established Ferrari owner even to buy the limited-use FXX, but by the end of 2005, more than 20 buyers stepped forward with their checkbooks.

End of the line? Still not yet, as in 2007 Ferrari announced the FXX Evolution for 2008.

By the time that the FXX Evolution came

FERRARI FXX

Price: $1.9 million

Engine: 789-horsepower, 6.3-liter V-12

0–60 mph: 2.8 seconds

Top speed: 217-plus mph

along in 2007, Ferrari engineers had pumped the power up to an impressive 860 at a screaming 9,500 rpm. Paddle shifts in the F1 gearbox take a mere 60 milliseconds.

Much of the development from the Enzo to the FXX was in the aerodynamics fitted to the carbon-fiber body. Where the FXX was an improvement over the Enzo, the Evolution is said to improve aero efficiency by an additional 25 percent. The brakes are large carbon ceramics from Brembo, while Bridgestone provides tires for the 19-inch alloy wheels.

Did You Know?

When Ferrari unveiled the FXX, it pegged the horsepower from the 6.3-liter V-12 at around 800 . . . and we can tell you it makes a mighty noise.

Just as Ford built the GT40 in the 1960s to beat Ferrari on the racetrack, it created the modern GT to best Ferrari's mid-engine V-8 street machines.

Designer Camilo Pardo stuck with the original shape of the GT40 when doing the GT, which is about 10 percent larger than the original. Ford's highly flexible 5.4-liter modular engine was chosen to power the exotic car, and the automaker made no secret that as the mid-engine chassis was developed, its target was Ferrari.

Although Ford built the engines and did the final assembly, the basic construction of the GTs was handled by Saleen in a factory in Troy, Michigan. Production began in 2004 and continued through 2006, by which time Ford had produced just over 4,000 GTs.

FORD GT

Price: $153,345
Engine: 550-horsepower, 5.4-liter, supercharged V-8
0–60 mph: 3.6 seconds
Top speed: 205 mph

Where Ferrari uses a 4.3-liter, 483-horsepower V-8 for its F430, Ford's V-8 displaces 5.4 liters and is supercharged via a Lysholm-type blower to 550 horsepower and 500 lb-ft of torque. The only gearbox offered with the Ford was a six-speed manual.

Just as the exterior design of Ford's GT mimicked the GT40, so too did the interior. That dashboard shape was the same as in the race cars, as was the pattern of the seat design. Great car to drive with that V-8 spinning behind you.

Did You Know?

Famed racer Steve Millen and his company, Stillen, turned a Ford GT into a serious rally/racing car. Horsepower was jumped to 630, and Millen reworked the suspension to turn the GT into a serious competition car, which he raced on the rugged Dunlop Targa New Zealand.

It was economic necessity that forced Lamborghini to keep the Countach in production for 16 years. When a deep-pockets savior came along, it was Chrysler Corporation. The Detroit company gave the Italian specialist the money and expertise it needed to create the Diablo for 1990.

To redo the exterior of its supercar, Lamborghini went back to Countach designer Marcello Gandini. His proposal wasn't quite what Chrysler wanted, and it was reworked by the automaker, which also did the interior.

LAMBORGHINI DIABLO

Price: $240,000 (1991)
Engine: 492-horsepower, 5.7-liter V-12
0–60 mph: 3.8 seconds
Top speed: 203 mph

Under the skin, much Countach remained, like the big size and the "backward" engine with the gearbox jutting forward into the passenger compartment.

In the end, the Diablo's lifespan covered 11 years, many special models, and the sale

of Lamborghini twice, finally to its current owner, Audi.

You feel a bit like a spaceship captain when driving a Diablo. You step over and settle down into the semi-reclining seat. Ahead of you is a tall instrument panel, while to your right the shift lever rises from the wide center console that hides the transmission.

Initially, the Diablo had a 5.7-liter V-12 with 492 horsepower. Special models took that as high as 595, but to keep things simple, the engine was enlarged for 2000 to 6.0 liters, which took horsepower to 550. Claimed top speeds were always over 200 but as high as 210 mph for some models.

Did You Know?

Like its predecessor, the Countach, and its successor, the Murciélago, the Diablo is a big machine, weighing in around 3,700 pounds. Still, there's plenty to motivate a Diablo with those 12 cylinders behind you, so 60 mph should come up in under 4.0 seconds.

LAMBORGHINI DIABLO

Lamborghini's Countach begat the Diablo, which begat the Murciélago. The cars have been developed through the years, but there is still a hint of Countach in the latest super-Lambo.

The exterior styling is as dramatic as ever. Same inside, where you slither down into laid-back seats with a tall transmission tunnel down the middle. It's tall in part because the V-12 fits "backward" in the mid-engine chassis, with the transmission forward of it, sticking into the cockpit. All part of Lambo's supercar image.

LAMBORGHINI MURCIÉLAGO LP640

Price: $313,600 (coupe), $345,000 (roadster)
Engine: 640-horsepower, 6.5-liter V-12
0–60 mph: 3.5 seconds
Top speed: 211 mph

Ah, yes, the heart of the matter: Lamborghini's powerful V-12. When the Murciélago was upgraded to LP640 status, the engine's displacement was enlarged to 6.5 liters, horsepower going to 640, torque

to 487 lb-ft. Transmitting that power to the low-profile tires is a six-speed manual transmission, optionally available with "E-gear" paddle shift.

Nothing says Lamborghini like swing-forward doors. First used commercially on the company's Countach, they remain an integral part of Lambo design. At speed, vents just above the rear tires swing out like batwings to gulp cooling air for the V-12.

Just when you begin to wonder, "what more could they do with the Murciélago design?" Lamborghini pops with the Reventon. Uncovered at the 2007 Frankfurt Auto Show, this gray, carbon-fiber version has a distinct anti-radar Stealth fighter look to it. Very slick . . . only 20 made and sold immediately.

Did You Know?

There is a racing version of the Murciélago called the R-GT. One nasty-looking race car, it has won FIA GT races, finally giving Lamborghini the racing victories it needs to cement its supercar reputation.

CY·802GV

Lamborghini

LAMBORGHINI GALLARDO

All of the many organizations that owned Lamborghini over the years promised a smaller, less-expensive model. This was a false pledge until Audi bought the Italian exotic firm in 1998.

It was worth the wait. While the Gallardo might be the Murciélago's little brother, it is arguably more fun to drive. For one thing, it's more manageable in size and more nimble. From its Audi parent, the small Lambo inherited an aluminum structure and body, so it's lightweight. Combine that with a very healthy V-10 with 520 horsepower and 376 lb-ft of torque, and you'll slam your way via all-wheel-drive to 60 mph in 3.8 seconds. That could be by way of a traditional six-speed manual gearbox or Lamborghini's E-gear manual automatic.

Guaranteed fun either way.

Sumptuous sportiness might be the best way to describe the Gallardo's interior. It has all the right stuff for a sports machine, like well-bolstered seats, good instrumentation, and the gearshift—lever or paddles—close at hand. And yet there's nothing spare or Spartan about this leather-upholstered cockpit.

LAMBORGHINI GALLARDO

Price: $201,000
Engine: 520-horsepower 5.0-liter V-10
0–60 mph: 3.8 seconds
Top speed: 196 mph

Did You Know?

Gallardos come with fixed metal or automatically folding soft tops. Hard to say which is more fun, though with the Spyder you get to hear the nicely raucous rasp of the V-10. That top can be raised or lowered in 20 seconds flat.

LOTUS ELISE

Just as certainly as we need to pay our respects to the big, booming exotic cars, we need to tip our hats to the lightweights. Not light in performance, but in weight.

The late Colin Chapman was the king of lightweight, and the firm he started, Lotus in England, still reigns as the champ of light.

As an example, we offer the Elise. Just 149.0 inches long on a 90.5-inch wheelbase, the little targa-style sports car (soft tops and hardtops available) weighs in at less than 2,000 pounds curb weight. The exterior design is a combo of cute, aggression, and distinction and is executed in RTM composite fiberglass—long a Lotus feature—over a chassis of epoxy-bonded aluminum extrusions.

For all the features and history a Lotus brings with it, prices are much more reasonable than the big bangers.

LOTUS ELISE

Price: $44,460
Engine: 190-horsepower, 1.8-liter inline four
0–60 mph: 4.7 seconds
Top speed: 150 mph

That's a modified Toyota engine slung sideways in the back of the Elise. The 1.8-liter engine is tuned to 190 horsepower and 134 lb-ft of torque. The gearbox is a six-speed manual, and the powertrain will scoot the light machine to 60 mph in 4.7 seconds, to 100 in 12.9, and then to 150 mph.

Inside, things are kept simple, but that's a good thing, a design element of a Lotus. Seats are in cloth, and there's plenty of leather and/or aluminum trim as standard or in option packages.

Did You Know?

Also on the options list is a Track Pack that includes a highly adjustable suspension.

Think of Lotus's Exige S as a super Elise . . . make that supercharged. Lotus takes the 1.8-liter four-cylinder engine, adds a driven supercharger, ups horsepower to 220, and drops 0–60-mph time to 4.1 seconds and 0–100 to 11.0.

You can't deny the Exige S has a purposeful look, sitting on its wheels with a ready-to-run stance.

This isn't a car you'd necessarily choose for coast-to-coast cruising, but it's perfect as a close-to-home dual-purpose machine that allows commuting during the week and competition on the weekends.

Lotus adds a Roots-type supercharger to the 1.8-liter Toyota-based engine in the Exige S, kicking horsepower up by 16 percent to 220, with torque jumping to 165 lb-ft.

LOTUS EXIGE S

Price: $59,890
Engine: 220-horsepower, 1.8-liter inline four
0–60 mph: 4.1 seconds
Top speed: 148 mph

Power then flows through a six-speed, close-ratio, manual gearbox.

Some might think the Exige S interior looks a bit Spartan, but that goes with the Lotus approach to light weight and efficiency equaling speed. It even has hand crank–driven window lifts and cloth seats. Those truly serious about weight-saving can cut 20 pounds (and $250) by deleting the air conditioning.

That wing is one of the things that sets

the Exige S apart from the Elise. It is just part of the aero package developed for the Exige—like the front splitter—to increase downforce. As with every Lotus for decades, the body is done in composite fiberglass.

Did You Know?

The options list allows buyers to turn this Lotus into a junior luxury sports car using the Touring pack with its leather upholstery, a better sound system, and added soundproofing. Or the Track Pack goes the other way, including adjustable Bilstein shocks. You can also add a limited-slip differential and traction control.

MASERATI MC12

After Ferrari had built its allotted 400 Enzos, the same carbon-fiber monocoque tub was inherited by corporate stablemate Maserati. Looking to improve its sporting image, Maser called the car MC12 and during 2004 and 2005 built 50 examples to be sold to customers.

MASERATI MC12

Price: $795,000
Engine: 630-horsepower, 6.0-liter V-12
0–60 mph: 3.5 seconds
Top speed: 205 mph

Also shared with the Enzo was the V-12 engine (now at 630 horsepower), the gearbox, and the upper and lower A-arm suspensions. Maserati did its own carbon-fiber bodywork—thanks to American designer Frank Stephenson—which gives the car its distinctive Maser looks. Unlike the Enzo, the MC12 has a removable targa top.

Pirelli supplied the tires, which measure 245/35R-19 front and 345/35R-19 rear and are mounted to aluminum alloy wheels. Inside are large Brembo disc brakes with

ABS. World Driving Champion Michael Schumacher was one of the drivers involved in developing the MC12's handling.

Where the Enzo's interior is all function with an emphasis on carbon-fiber, the MC12's inside is downright luxurious. There's a combination of aluminum, leather, and a fabric called BrighTex. Detailing includes a vintage-looking analog clock. Even the Enzo-derived seats are nicely upholstered.

Maserati's race version of the MC12 is called the GT1. When the company competed with the car in the American and European Le Mans series, it ran afoul of the rules, being too wide. However, MC12 GT1s race in the European FIA GT1 class and won the manufacturer's trophy in 2005, 2006, and 2007.

Did You Know?

At 630 horsepower, the MC12's V-12 has 20 less than the Enzo, but the Maser is also 100 pounds lighter, so the car's performance is similar. You fire up the Maserati's V-12 by pushing a blue START button.

L4 13275

MCLAREN F1

Gordon Murray is one of the most brilliant automotive designers. Creator of several winning Grand Prix designs, Murray asked Ron Dennis, boss of the McLaren Formula 1 team, for the chance to build the perfect road-going sports car. The result is the McLaren F1.

Small (168.8 inches long) and light (2,513 pounds) and powerful (627 horsepower), the F1 can get to 60 mph in 3.2 seconds, to 200 mph in 28 seconds, and on to a top speed of 245 mph.

Drawing on his race car experience, Murray used carbon-fiber for the F1's monocoque chassis and bodywork, also employing such lightweight materials as titanium and magnesium.

The result is arguably the most desirable exotic car in the world, its value today

MCLAREN F1

Price: $890,000 (when new)
Engine: 627-horsepower, 6.1-liter V-12
0–60 mph: 3.2 seconds
Top speed: 245 mph

around $1.2 million.

Credit for the exterior design of the F1 goes to both Gordon Murray and designer Peter Stevens. The shape is a combination of function and beauty, one of Murray's goals being no exterior aerodynamic devices . . . they are hidden inside the bodywork. Only 100 F1s, including the racing versions, were built between 1993 and 1998.

Originally, Gordon Murray contacted Honda about an engine for the McLaren, but it was BMW Motorsports that created the custom-built V-12 for the F1. Murray asked for 550 horsepower, but BMW delivered 627 from the 6.1 liters of the aluminum engine. Torque is an equally impressive 480 lb-ft. The car's transverse gearbox was designed in the United States.

Did You Know?

The most striking feature of the McLaren's interior is the center seat for the driver. It may be a bit difficult to climb in there, but once seated, it gives what many call the perfect position in a high-speed machine. And riding along is quite a treat for passengers to the driver's right and left.

NEW YORK
RLONE
THE EMPIRE STATE

McLaren
M Power

Although the McLaren F1 wasn't originally meant to be a race car, several customers of the supercar wanted to compete, so McLaren created racing versions. In its first attempt—1995—McLaren not only won the 24 Hours of Le Mans, but F1s also finished 3rd, 4th, 5th, and 13th.

To mark this amazing feat, McLaren built five special models called F1 LM (for Le Mans). Again, the BMW V-12 was the powerplant, but while it had all the race car specifications, it didn't need the inlet air restrictors demanded by Le Mans. The resulting 680 horsepower is the most in any McLaren F1, road or track.

McLaren kept all the winning race car's aerodynamics for the road-going F1 LM, the most noticeable the tall rear wing. Stripped of the amenities needed to make it a civilized road car, the LM is about 120 pounds lighter than the street version.

As in the race cars, the F1 LMs were built without the soundproofing used in the road machines. So those noise-canceling headphones seen at the right are mandatory for driver and passengers to communicate. There is generous use of carbon-fiber for light weight, and many standard switches were replaced with functional toggles.

In the only recorded road test of an F1 LM, famed race driver Andy Wallace took

MCLAREN F1 LM

Price: $1,200,000 (when new)
Engine: 680-horsepower, 6.1-liter V-12
0–60 mph: est. 3.0 seconds
Top speed: est. 250 mph

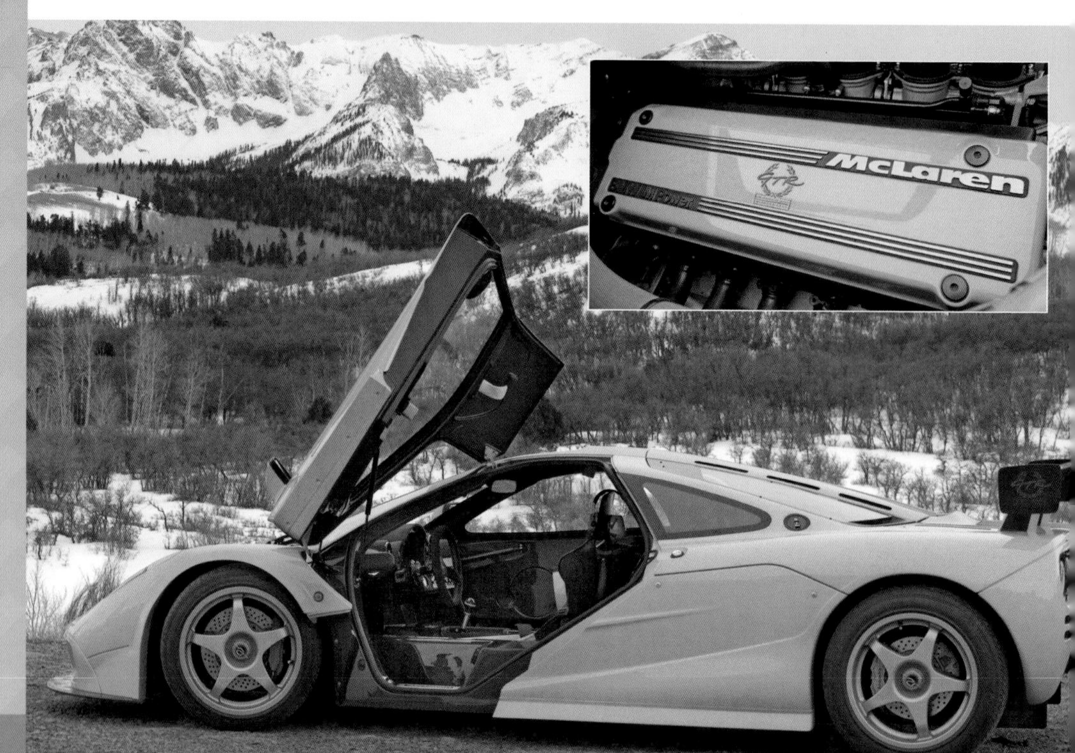

one of the orange street racers from 0 to 100 mph and back to 0 in just 11.5 seconds. This particular F1 LM is owned by designer Ralph Lauren, who also has a normal F1 . . . if normal could ever describe a McLaren F1.

Did You Know?

In memory of the company's founder, the late race driver Bruce McLaren, all F1 LMs are painted his signature color: Papaya Orange.

PAGANI ZONDA

Horace Pagani moved from his native Argentina to Italy, became an expert in the then-new process of carbon-fiber, and decided to use it to make his own automobiles. Sounds a bit ambitious, doesn't it? And yet for the past near decade, Pagani automobiles have been produced in a small factory near Modena, not far from Ferrari and Lamborghini.

In that time, there have been maybe 75 Pagani Zondas produced. They've come in several forms, coupe and spyder, and with various states of tune of their powerplant,

PAGANI ZONDA

Price: $350,000 (C 12 S)
Engine: 555-horsepower, 7.3-liter V-12
0–60 mph: 3.5 seconds
Top speed: 220 mph

Mercedes-Benz's AMG V-12. What hasn't changed much is the rather dramatic bodywork, which was designed by Pagani himself and is done almost completely in carbon-fiber.

Pagani rather sensibly relies on Mercedes

via AMG for his powerplants. It's always the V-12, and he has used it in 6.0-, 7.0-, and 7.3-liter forms. Horsepower has ranged from just over 400 horsepower to just over 600 horsepower, which is quite good considering the cars tend to weigh right around 2,750 pounds.

Pagani interiors are always interesting, with seats that are dramatically formed in a layout that has an almost art deco look to it. Note the pedals, the steering wheel, and the shape of the instruments. Nail that gas pedal, and most Paganis will get you to 60 mph in less than 4.0 seconds.

Dramatic enough for you? While it can be argued that the exterior shape of the Pagani isn't as sophisticated as a Ferrari, it certainly is as exciting. More so with the Roadster, which was introduced at the 2006 Geneva Auto Show. Pagani claims the open-top car is as rigid as the coupe and weighs the same.

Did You Know?

As you might guess, Paganis aren't cheap, the price eating up much of a $500,000 bank account, but you can't fault the cars for exclusivity.

MERCEDES-BENZ
PAGANI
Roadster

PAGANI ZONDA

PORSCHE CAYMAN S

Some cars just work perfectly as a total package, and that includes Porsche's Cayman S. The look is just right, combining elements of the venerable 911, the upstart Boxster roadster, and Porsche history.

Like all Porsches, the Cayman was developed to be a driver's car but has advantages over its stablemates. Unlike the Boxster, it is a closed design, so it could be designed with a stiffer chassis, actually 2.5 times more so in torsion than in the open machine. Unlike the 911, which has been developed into a fine-handling car despite its rear engine placement, the Cayman has a mid-engine, all the better for balance.

Porsche created the 3.4-liter flat six in the Cayman S from the 3.2-liter powerplant in the Boxster. As nice as the 295 horsepower is, the 251 lb-ft of torque, helps account for the quick 0–60 and 0–100 times. The wing automatically deploys at 75 mph and retracts at 50 mph.

Anyone who knows Porsche interiors will recognize the Cayman S. The gauge layout is Boxster-like, and things are a bit more stylish than the 911. And being a Porsche, you can bet the seats will be as good at holding you in place during hard cornering as supporting you on a long drive.

PORSCHE CAYMAN S

Price: $60,000

Engine: 295-horsepower, 3.4-liter flat six

0–60 mph: 4.8 seconds

Top speed: 170 mph

Did You Know?

Backing up the basic suspension design is Porsche Active Suspension Management, which can alter the handling characteristics from road to track but also save your bacon if you overdo things on the twisty bits.

PORSCHE TURBO

Saying "Turbo" in front of many Porsche fanatics is like throwing raw meat to starving lions. It's what they live for, just as they have for the past 30 years.

And the legend continues, now with 480 horsepower and a 0–60 time of only 3.6 seconds. This power is doled out through all-wheel drive and the sophisticated Porsche Traction Management system that uses a multiplate clutch system to send power to the wheels with the best traction.

And to go with the power, Porsche gives the Turbo the sort of nice-to-be-nasty looks that prove it means business.

Porsche is finally putting some design time into making its engine compartments look better, but what really makes this photo sing is hard to read. It's the "Variable Turbine Geometry" wording that refers to the Turbos' ability to adjust their vanes as rpm climbs.

It's all those vents that give the Turbo its serious business look . . . and with good reason—actually the 480 reasons that represent the horsepower and the 457-to-502 that refer to the lb-ft of torque. That torque variability comes with the Sport Chrono Package that gives the driver a 10-second power burst thanks to a temporarily added 2.9 psi of boost.

It's the five-dial grouping of gauges that immediately marks this as a 911 from Porsche. Off to the right is the center stack, which contains such important functions as audio controls, heating and A/C buttons, and the navigational system. Those seats sit as good as they look.

PORSCHE TURBO

Price: $122,900 (2007)
Engine: 480-horsepower, 3.6-liter, twin-turbo flat six
0–60 mph: 3.6 seconds
Top speed: 193 mph

Did You Know?

During the fuel and emissions crisis years of the mid-1970s, Porsche breathed new life into its already aging 911 with turbochargers. It applied the technology to racing and created a generation of all-conquering race cars.

PORSCHE 911 GT3 RS

Those letters "RS" stand for *Rennsport,* German for "Racing Sport," and this 911 is well named. Get in, sit down in the form-fitting seat, belt up snuggly, and turn the key. The flat six growls alive behind you. While many modern supercars have paddle-shifter transmissions, a Porsche still feels best with a traditional manual gearbox. Slot it into first, and off you go.

This is not a subtle machine. You probably wouldn't want to drive it from Los Angeles to New York, but get it on a fast, twisting road, and it's a wonder car. *Bam,* first gear to second, *bam,* on to third . . . 100 mph covered in just 10.7 seconds, soaking up turns beneath you. Hey, that's why they call it a Rennsport.

Lift the rear engine cover of a 911, and you won't find beauty, but who cares? Crammed low in that tight space is Porsche's famous flat six, now opened up to 3.6 liters and urging the GT3 RS on with 415 horsepower and 300 lb-ft of torque.

Where some automakers seem to delight in changing their interior with each new model, Porsche profits from not doing so. The familiar gauge layout is as good as it was decades ago, so why change? That stripe at the top of the steering wheel is to remind drivers where they are in the wheel's arc as they rush along.

PORSCHE 911 GT3 RS

Price: $123,200
Engine: 415-horsepower, 3.6-liter flat six
0–60 mph: 3.9 seconds
Top speed: 192 mph

Did You Know?

Okay, it looks very cool, but this rear wing, like the detailing of the GT3 RS's nose, is the result of serious wind tunnel work. Give a car like this a 3.9-seconds-to-60-mph punch off the line and a top speed of 192 mph, and you need to pay attention to its aerodynamics.

PORSCHE CARRERA GT

PORSCHE CARRERA GT

Price: $440,000 (2005)
Engine: 605-horsepower, 5.7-liter V-10
0–60 mph: 3.6 seconds
Top speed: 205 mph

Produced in Porsche's Leipzig factory alongside the Cayenne, the Carrera is assembled from modules—several made in Italy—that attach to a carbon-fiber/aluminum-honeycomb monocoque. It's an impressive process to watch as the snail-like line inches forward and GTs are completed.

When finished, you have an exciting exterior design that could only be a Porsche from its low, wide mouth and flared headlamps back to its taillights and spoiler. Ditto inside with a combo of leather and brushed aluminum with a hint of carbon-fiber.

Suspensions under the Carrera GT have the expected upper and lower A-arm pushrod designs. The brakes are unusual in being the same size front and rear with a 15.0-inch diameter. Michelin Pilot Sports are the standard tire, measuring 265/35ZR-19 front and 335/30ZR-19 at the back.

Under that beautifully sculpted engine cover is the V-10 that began life as a Formula 1 design, was then proposed as a Le Mans engine, temporarily abandoned, and then was brought to life with 5.7 liters for the Carrera GT. For the street, it has a claimed 605 horsepower and 435 lb-ft of torque. The transmission has seven speeds, a traditional manual shift, and an advanced ceramic-composite clutch.

Did You Know?

Porsche began a program in the late 1990s to build a new race car for the 24 Hours of Le Mans. It pulled the plug on the idea but kept the design in hand, reviving it for a new supercar to rival such machines as Ferrari's Enzo and Bugatti's Veyron.

SALEEN S7

Steve Saleen had been building super Mustangs for years when he decided to get into the supercar business. The Irvine, California, company designed what is basically a civilized race car and introduced it in 2000. The chassis has a mid-engine layout and is formed from steel and aluminum honeycomb panels. The dramatic body was designed by Phil Frank, was tuned in the wind tunnel, and is done in carbon-fiber.

Inside is a race car interior, except that it is finished off like a luxury car, with leather upholstery and luxo detailing on the dashboard.

When driving a Saleen, you have to remember its race car basics, but those come back to you in this solid, highly competent machine as the speed rises.

Under that sleek bodywork is a chassis that is a successful runner on tracks like Le Mans and Sebring. The suspension has upper and lower A-arms all around and, like a race car, is adjustable. Big disc brakes haul you down from speed, while those squat tires hold you fast to the pavement.

Given its race-car-for-the-street nature, it wasn't surprising when racing versions called S7-Rs proved successful on the track. Saleens have been raced more extensively in Europe than in the United States, though they did score a class win in the 12 Hours of Sebring. Saleens have won numerous European FIA GT events.

SALEEN S7

Price: $555,000 (2006)
Engine: 750-horsepower, 7.0-liter, twin-turbo V-8
0–60 mph: 3.3 seconds
Top speed: 248 mph

Did You Know?

Initially, S7s were fitted with 7-liter, Ford-based, aluminum V-8s with 550 horsepower and 525 lb-ft of torque, which would seem to be enough for a car that weighs just 2,750 pounds. Then Saleen went one better, adding a pair of turbochargers to rocket the power to 750 horsepower and 700 lb-ft of torque.

RUF RT12

Call Alois Ruf the magician of Pfaffenhausen, Germany. For decades, the engine wizard has been transforming already potent Porsches into supercars.

The latest magic from Ruf is the Rt12, which can be had in basic form for $250,000, though options can more than double that cost. Ruf redoes his cars' bodywork, not for glitz, but to refine the aerodynamics to deal with the forces exerted on the car at its 200-plus-mph top speed. The result is cars that are beautifully functional.

RUF RT12

Price: $650,000
Engine: 3.8-liter, twin-turbo flat six, 650 horsepower
0–60 mph: 3.2 seconds
Top speed: 219 mph

Inside are Ruf's own seats, which are shaped to cope with the car's potential and yet are quite comfortable.

In addition to reworking the engine, Ruf makes certain the rest of the car is up to the

greater *umph*! of the engine. The suspension is reworked to be firmer, though it's not rock hard. When the car accelerates, you can feel the Rt12's stiff body twist a bit from the mega-torque.

Punch the throttle of the 650-horsepower Rt12, and in just 3.2 seconds that speedo needle will swing past 60 mph. Stay with the power, and before the rev counter is at maximum rpm, the speedometer gauge will be reading just shy of 220 mph.

Rt12s can be had with either of three flat-six twin-turbocharged engines. Two have 3.6-liter displacements and 530 or 560 horsepower, while the upgrade has 3.8 liters and 650 horsepower. The gearbox is a six-speed manual and can work though rear drive or all-wheel drive.

Did You Know?

Ruf's conversions are so complete the cars are no longer officially Porsches but are certified by the German government as Rufs.

Consider
remaining
range
MN RT 12

Although the Spyker name is new to most car fans, it was actually used on a nicely engineered machine before World War I. That car was produced in the Netherlands, so when a new car was designed and developed there, the owners took on the earlier name.

The Spyker team created a compact, high-performance sports car that measures just 164.8 inches long on a 101.4-inch wheelbase. The exterior design is controversial, not particularly pretty but certainly purposeful with all its louvers and ducts. Inside is a very pretty, highly detailed interior . . . lots of what designers call "jewelry."

Audi supplies the car's 4.2-liter V-8, the same used in the S4, and it is combined with a six-speed manual, the duo in the 3,000-pound car enough not just to get it to

SPYKER C8

Price: $269,995
Engine: 400-horsepower, 4.2-liter V-8
0–60 mph: 4.4 seconds
Top speed: 150 mph

60 mph in 4.4 seconds but take it on to 100 mph in 10.3 seconds.

Try to say "Spyker Spyder" very fast a dozen times. Tough, isn't it? On this open version, the design has a more integrated look to it with the cooling louvers and the chrome intake ducts blending nicely with the color.

Anyone who knows Formula 1 also knows that Spyker had a Grand Prix team, though it was sold after the 2007 season. The company has also raced the C8, as seen on the next page at the 2007 24 Hours of Le Mans.

Did You Know?

The next Spyker? At the 2007 Geneva Auto Show, the Dutch company previewed the new version called the C12 (next page, lower right), enveloped in a body by the well-known Italian design firm Zagato. The concept retains the window-in-a-window feature in the flip-up doors.

86
LEMO
LeasePlan
www.spykercars.com
MICHELIN
MOTON
McGREGOR
86

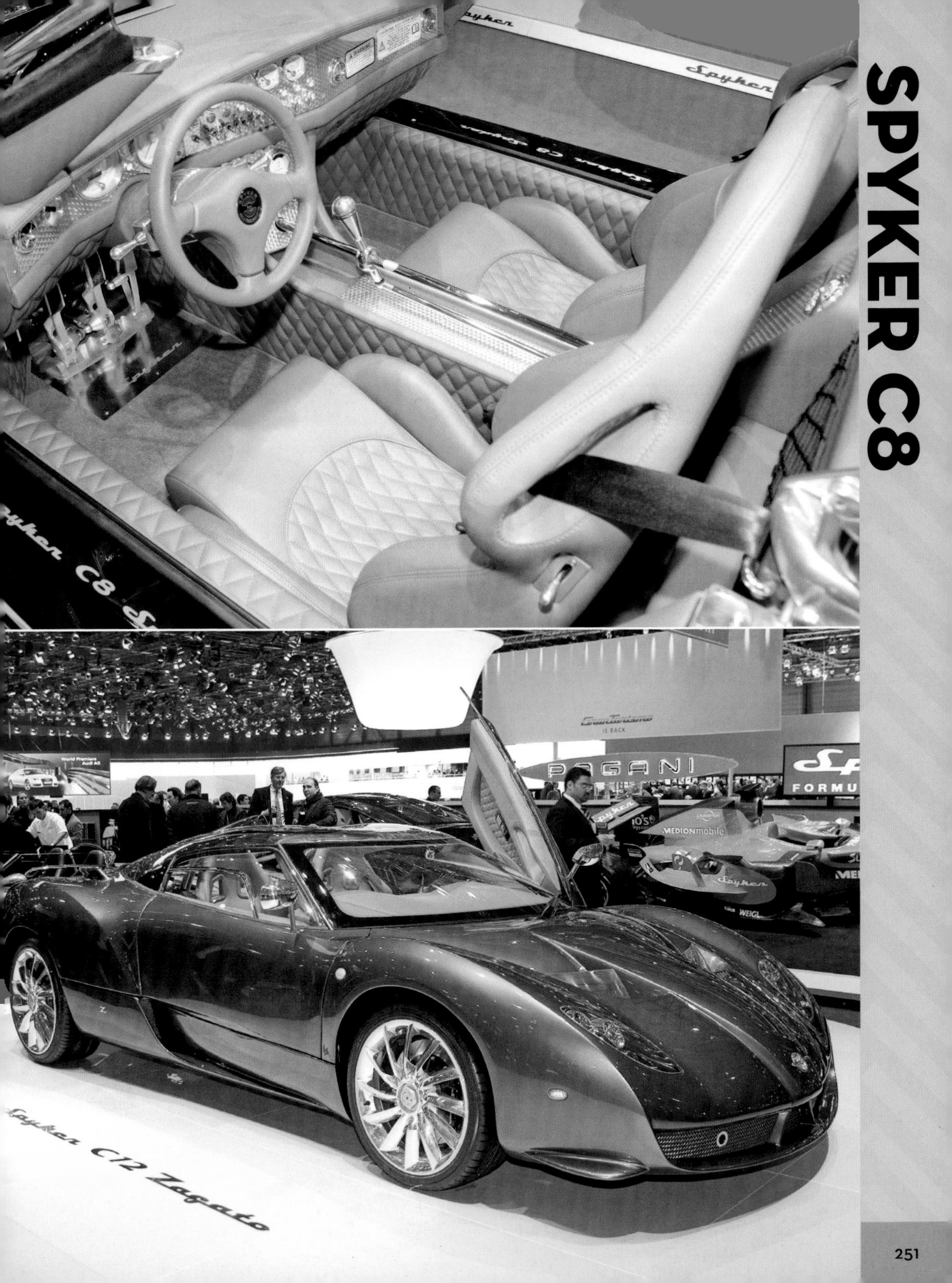
Spyker
Spyker C8 Spyker
Spyker C8
World Premiere Audi A5
PAGANI
FORMU
MEDIONmobile
WEIGL
Spyker C12 Zagato

VECTOR AVTECH WX8

To be honest, the history of Vector supercars reads more like a soap opera than an automotive story. And like a good soap opera, it reads like a story with no end.

Back in the 1970s, designer Gerald Wiegert created a shape for a new exotic car that was undeniably heart-stopping. Low, wide, and well-muscled, the Vectors were made from all-American materials and were said to reflect jet fighter technology. Road tests in 1992 showed 0–60 times in 4.3 seconds, which was remarkable at the time.

After all the years, however, few cars were built and sold, and the Vector story seemed to unravel in the mid-1990s.

Not so fast. At the 2007 Los Angeles Auto Show, what should be tucked off in a corner but the Vector Avtech WX8.

Who knows, maybe the Vector story isn't over . . .

VECTOR AVTECH WX8

Price: est. $450,000

Engine: 600- to 700-horsepower, 7.0-liter V-8

0–60 mph: est. 3.3 seconds

Top speed: est. 270 mph

Vectors never wanted for power, which is again provided by a U.S. big-block 7.0-liter V-8. Featuring titanium valves, the engine comes in two basic forms: normally aspirated and supercharged. Horsepower for the former is said to be 600–700, while the blown version can be taken to 1,200 horsepower. The 0–60-mph times are claimed to be 3.0–3.3 seconds, the top speed above 270 mph.

look and feel of an
Advanced Tactical Fighter (ATF) aircraft.

Did You Know?

The basic dramatic Vector shape is still there but now with more swoops, vents, air ducts, and spoilers. The body is made of carbon-fiber/E-glass structural panels. Inside, the theme is again taken from jet fighters, the instrument panel hewn from billet aluminum and fitted with what Vector says are "military specification F-22 Raptor switches."

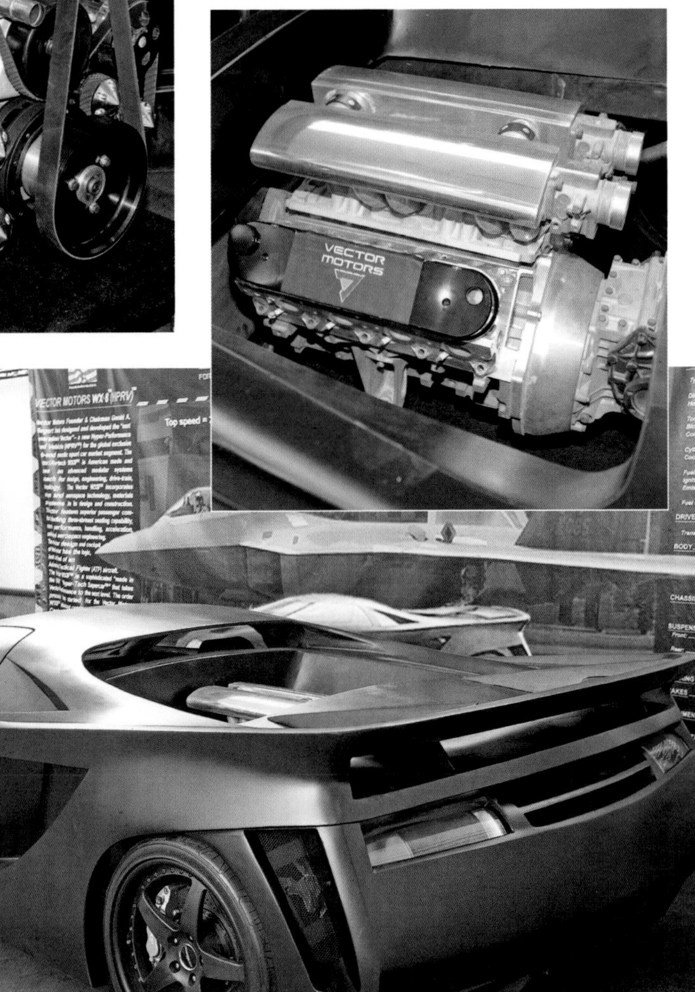

INDEX